SUMMER
A European play

Published to coincide with the premiere
January 1982, *Summer* is set in Eastern I   ing
the sea. The play centres on an encount   ...о.., whose pasts are
terribly bound up with the German wartime occupation of the town and nearby
islands. Forty years ago, Xenia's family threw dinner parties for the German
officers in that very house; Marthe, the family servant, was taken prisoner along
with many of the townspeople and condemned to be shot. Only Xenia's
intervention saved Marthe's life.

But now, Xenia lives in England and Marthe still lives in the house. Xenia's visit –
and the news that Marthe is dying of an incurable disease – provokes a searing
reappraisal of the meaning of the past events and of the present.

SUMMER

by

EDWARD BOND

A Methuen New Theatrescript
Methuen · London

This is the script of the play as it was before rehearsals for the first production. It must not be taken as the basis for future productions. A definitive, post-production version of the play will be published by Methuen Modern Plays in due course.

First published in Great Britain in 1982 by Methuen London Ltd,
11 New Fetter Lane, London EC4P 4EE

ISBN 0 413 4932 02
       0 413 49329 6 (National Theatre edition only)

Characters

MARTHE
XENIA
ANN

DAVID
GERMAN

VOICES, *heard*

Scenes

1. House. Night
2. House. Morning.
3. House. Afternoon
4. Island. Late afternoon.
5. House. Night.
6. House. Morning.
7. House. Late morning.

The present.
Eastern Europe.

The terrace of a cliff house facing the sea.
Down right a door leads downstairs to the street.
Up right a door leads upstairs to other parts of the house.
In the wall at the back, left, a door leads to a room.
Left, railings face the sea.

One

The house. Night.
DAVID *comes in with* XENIA *and* ANN.
He carries cases. XENIA *and* ANN *carry
hand luggage.*

DAVID: You're in your old room. I'm
sorry I couldn't meet you at the airport.

XENIA: It doesn't matter.

DAVID (*smiles*): I'd swapped with a
colleague to have the morning off.

XENIA: It wasn't your fault our plane was
late. We sat at Heathrow all day.

DAVID: I'll take these things up and fetch
the rest from below.

ANN: I'll help you.

DAVID: No no, I can manage. You must
be tired.

DAVID *goes.*

XENIA (*calling after him*): Where's
Marthe?

ANN (*glances round*): Nothing's changed.

XENIA: You don't know it as well as I do.
That hideous new hotel. A dreadful
holiday camp stood on end. I shouldn't
complain. People must have holidays. I'll
be all right tomorrow. Waiting at airports
always depresses me. It's so inefficient.
At least they've left the sea where it was.
(*She goes to the railing.*) Thank God you
don't see the hotel from here. You'll see it
from below.

DAVID *comes in with two cases. He nods
at a case already there.*

DAVID: I'll come back for that.

XENIA: Where's your mother?

DAVID: Resting.

XENIA: I suppose your new hotel has a
discotheque?

DAVID: Wednesdays and Saturdays.

DAVID *goes.* XENIA *follows him out.
She takes her hand luggage.* ANN *is
alone. She goes to the railing and looks at
the sea.* DAVID *comes back.*

DAVID (*points to the case*): Shall I put that
in your room?

ANN: Yes.

DAVID: I'm glad you're back.

ANN: Thank you.

DAVID: Are you tired?

ANN: A little.

DAVID: I have to work in the morning. I
have the afternoon off. I'll take you
swimming.

ANN: Thank you.

DAVID: I've arranged to have most of my
time off while you're here. I have to go in
some mornings to see a sick child.

XENIA (*off, calls*): Ann.

ANN (*calls*): Coming. (*To* DAVID:) You
mustn't inconvenience your colleagues
because of me.

DAVID: It's part of my holidays.

ANN *goes.* DAVID *is alone. He taps on
the rear door.*

(*Low:*) She's gone upstairs.

DAVID *sits. He stretches his legs in front
of him and broods. After a few moments
the door opens and* MARTHE *comes out.*

MARTHE: When I hear her voice it's as if
I'm back in the past.

DAVID: Why let her come?

MARTHE: I can't stop her. Anyone can
book the guest rooms.

DAVID: Say they're already booked.

MARTHE: Don't be a child. I don't mind
her.

DAVID: She upsets you. Let me send her
away.

MARTHE: It would be cruel to do it now.
Let things go on as before.

DAVID: As you please. But don't see her
tonight. That can wait till the morning.

MARTHE (*looks at the sea*): Yes, that
would be best.

ANN *comes in.*

ANN: Hello.

MARTHE: My dear. (*She kisses* ANN.)
Was it a dreadful journey?

ANN: The plane took off late. We had to
wait at the airport. We couldn't leave
because our flight could have been called
at any time.

XENIA (*off, calls*): Ann darling.

ANN: Excuse me. (*Calls:*) Yes?

XENIA (*off, calls*): Bring my keys. I want to undo my cases.

ANN (*calls*): I haven't got them.

XENIA (*off, calls*): I gave them to you when we left the house.

ANN (*calls*): They're in your handbag.

XENIA (*off, calls*): Oh no, you've left them behind. It's too much.

ANN (*calls*): Look in your handbag.

MARTHE (*moving towards her room*): Will you want anything to eat?

ANN: No, we've been eating all day.

MARTHE: You look well.

ANN: Thank you.

MARTHE: A little pale. You'll soon catch the sun. Till the morning. We'll breakfast together.

MARTHE *goes into her room and shuts the door.*

DAVID: Has she lost her keys?

ANN: I don't know. Anyway a lot of her things are in my cases.

DAVID: How's your father?

ANN: Always the same. He's on a diet. He's been on it for years. He enjoys having the house to himself while we're away.

DAVID: I thought you were a happy family.

ANN: We are. We never quarrel. I meant it must be nice when there's no one to bump into.

DAVID: Shall I come to your room tonight?

ANN: No, if you don't mind. The journey's tired me.

DAVID: It's all right. You'll feel better after you've slept. Would your mother like a drink?

ANN: I'll ask when I go up.

DAVID: Is anything wrong?

ANNA: Oh, please. I've been travelling with strangers all day. Surely it's natural for me to want to be quiet? It doesn't mean I'm ill, does it? Why must you – intrude all the time?

DAVID: You've grown very beautiful this year.

XENIA *comes in.*

XENIA: I was in the hallway at the foot of the stairs. Just before we left the house. Daddy had brought the car to the front. I gave them to you and went back to make sure Timmy was shut in the kitchen. You remember?

ANN: No.

XENIA: It's too much. On top of everything. Sometimes one can't rely on you at all. Have you looked for them?

ANN: I haven't got them.

XENIA: Give me your bag. (*She looks in ANN's travelling bag. She finds keys.*) These are yours?

ANN: Yes.

XENIA: How absurd. I'll have to break the locks. The three cases will be ruined. Shops won't replace locks on cases anymore. David, have you got any case keys?

DAVID: Yes, in my room.

XENIA: Did you buy your cases in the West?

DAVID: No.

XENIA: Then your keys won't fit my locks. Please bring me a hammer and a robust screwdriver.

DAVID: No. It's silly to break them. I'll get some keys for you to try in the morning. Ann or my mother will lend you what you need till then.

XENIA: I like to feel at home in this house – unpack my things and hang them in their place. Now there's all this muddle. I might as well be in a hotel.

DAVID: You've had a bad day.

XENIA: Well, at least Ann brought her own keys. We must be grateful she didn't leave them behind with mine. It will do me good to put up with the inconvenience. I'm not a good traveller. I don't know why Ann travels with me. If we had the same luggage your keys would have fitted mine. Have you looked in your pockets?

ANN: You didn't give me your keys.

XENIA: Well, if you did put them in your pocket they'll have dropped out in the plane or the airport, so I hope you didn't.

DAVID: Would you like a drink?

XENIA: I'm surprised they didn't build the hotel on one of the islands. Yes, I know the islands are a national monument. That wouldn't stop them. Can you still bathe from these rocks?

DAVID: Why not?

XENIA: Doesn't the hotel litter float by?

DAVID: The odd ice cream carton.

XENIA: I shall telephone Daddy in the morning and ask him to look for my keys on the hall table. I hope he doesn't find them before I telephone.

DAVID: A military man would survive the shock.

XENIA: It isn't a question of shock. It would distress him to know I had been unable to open my cases after a tiring journey. That's why I want to reassure him I'm not upset. It's a question of two people caring for one another.

ANN: I don't see the point of knowing they're on the hall table.

XENIA: If I know they're there I won't spend the whole of the holiday worrying about them. Are the telephones working?

DAVID: Yes.

XENIA: They didn't two years ago.

DAVID: That was after the hurricane.

XENIA: So it was. Where's Marthe?

DAVID: In her room.

XENIA: Is she unwell?

DAVID: She lives down here now.

XENIA: Why?

DAVID: To be next to the terrace. She sits there during the day.

XENIA: What's the matter? She's ill.

DAVID: Yes.

XENIA: Seriously? I must go to her.

DAVID: You'll see her in the morning. She needs rest.

XENIA: But what's the matter with her? Why didn't you tell me before?

DAVID: I didn't have a chance.

XENIA: Nonsense. You could have told me down in the street.

DAVID: She has a reticulosis.

XENIA: What's that? Please don't confuse me with medical jargon.

DAVID: It's a disease of the lymphatic glands.

XENIA: Is it serious?

DAVID: Yes, it's terminal.

XENIA: But she'll get better?

DAVID: No.

XENIA: You think she . . . ?

DAVID: Yes.

XENIA: David what are you telling me? Surely there's a cure? (*Panic whisper:*) Dear God, can she hear us? Really David I think you might have told me sooner. That ridiculous fuss about my keys.

DAVID: It doesn't matter. Please don't upset yourself.

XENIA: Of course I'm upset. It's a terrible shock.

DAVID: Yes.

XENIA: Is there no cure?

DAVID: No.

XENIA: Oh God. Is she in pain? Our holiday is off. You should have written and told me.

DAVID: She wouldn't let me write. You'd have come anyway.

XENIA: Certainly, to nurse her – or help in some other way. You must tell me what to do.

DAVID: Don't strain her. Just behave as you normally would.

XENIA: Of course, of course. How long will it take? You can't possibly know. Tell me the worst so I'm prepared. Is she in pain? Can she walk?

DAVID: You won't see much change so far. She has no pain. We've known for six weeks she was dying. I don't know how much longer she'll live. It doesn't shock her now. She knows it's true.

XENIA: Are you treating her?

DAVID: Yes.

XENIA: David, I'm so sorry.

DAVID: Yes, it's very sad.

XENIA: She's lucky to have you. You will tell me what I can do? Nursing, washing, anything.

DAVID: Thank you, but there is nothing.

XENIA: And you, if we can help you in any way. It's terrible for you. You are so close. We mustn't stay here gossiping. She must have rest and quiet.

DAVID: You've forgotten what else I said. Please behave as you normally would. Otherwise you'll frighten her and aggravate her condition.

XENIA: Yes, of course. David, Goodnight. Ann, come with me.

DAVID: Goodnight.

XENIA *goes.* ANN *looks at* DAVID *and then follows her mother out. He sits hunched in the chair and empties his mind.*

Two

The house. Morning.
MARTHE *sits in her chair up left.*
XENIA *comes in.*

XENIA: Marthe.

MARTHE: Hello. How are you? (XENIA *kisses her.*)

XENIA: Oughtn't you to lie down? I'm surprised David lets you sit out here.

MARTHE: Did you sleep well?

XENIA: Would you expect me to? I was so tired when I arrived. We'd spent all day at Heathrow. After David told me you were ill I hardly slept at all. He seems very pessimistic about this lymphatic-thing. Sometimes doctors almost sound proud of the diseases they're treating. They like to look on the dark side so that they can claim a miracle cure. It's good for their reputation even if it's bad for their patients. Let me get you a shawl.

MARTHE: I'd be far too hot.

XENIA: My mother moved into that room whenever she was ill.

MARTHE: So she did. I'd forgotten.

XENIA: Fortunately I can stay on this year till you're better. Ann will look after the boutique. It's time she learned to stand on her own feet. I can keep in touch by telephone. I'll have to go back for the spring buy but that won't –

MARTHE: I can't disrupt your life like that.

XENIA: Well, I've offered. I hope you change your mind.

MARTHE: Thank you. We'll see.

XENIA: What d'you do all day?

MARTHE: I can still do a little work. Mostly I sit and look at the sea.

XENIA: I don't like to see you resigned like this. You seem to have given in. You're still young, your life is worth saving. How can you be sure nothing can be done? Because David's your son I suppose you find it hard to believe he's wrong. Doctors do make mistakes – more than the rest of us. Who made the diagnosis? Have you taken a second opinion?. Has David discussed your treatment with a specialist?

MARTHE: Everything was done as it should be.

XENIA: Modern medicine moves so fast. They do things now that would have been miracles a few years ago. If you'd telephoned I'd have brought drugs from England. I don't know how up-to-date David's clinic is or if they have any equipment. He'd be cross if I asked.

MARTHE: He does all that can be done for me. Which isn't hard – there's very little. Did you find your keys?

XENIA: I knew my shouting woke you last night.

MARTHE: I wasn't asleep.

XENIA: David said he would get me some keys this morning. Oh let's not worry about the wretched things. Do you have pain?

MARTHE: No. I get tired, but that's more mental than physical. The strain.

XENIA: Come to England. David has money. And Bertie and I would help. A gift – or a loan if you wished. You could go to a private clinic for a check-up.

Surely David wouldn't stop you. I've seen other people in your situation. You'll leave it and make up your mind when it's late. Then they'd have to bring you in a wheelchair. Another excuse for them to do nothing: the journey would be too tiring.

MARTHE: David says nothing can be done.

XENIA: He can't know that. I've been told not to tire you so I'll be careful. But at least I can ask you to take a fresh look at yourself. That can't do any harm! Fight. Don't sit in a chair and wait. I'm glad I didn't know you were ill before I came. I can see what's happening with a fresh mind. You're all so apathetic. You've resigned yourself as if you were meeting fate. It's not like you. A doctor's word isn't law.

MARTHE: I don't want to die.

XENIA: At least you can still talk sense. I'm sorry, but you're irresponsible. It's criminal to stay here. If you went you'd have a chance.

ANN *comes in.*

ANN (*showing two large hoops of keys*): Look. (*She kisses* XENIA.)

MARTHE: Good heavens, there must be hundreds.

ANN (*kisses* MARTHE): Hello. I borrowed them from the hotel.

XENIA: Obviously they hadn't heard of your way with keys.

ANN: David came with me. I'll go and try them. Cross your fingers.

XENIA: Don't force the locks.

ANN *goes.*

All this fuss. If they're broken they're broken. I'll get some cheap ones in town to last till I get home. You can have the old ones. Perhaps you can still get locks fitted here. If not they'll be useful for something. She slept with David last year. Obviously he'll be thinking about other things now. Has he a steady girl? Most young doctors seem to have several unsteady ones. Ann would never live here.

MARTHE: Has she said?

XENIA: Oh she knows too much about the past. It would be a terrible wrong to a child to force it to fight its parents' battles. We do them enough harm without that. I've never forced my views on her. I've simply told her the truth. Children have a right to know the world they're in. I showed her the spot that used to be the library where her grandfather was arrested. I showed her the walls of the prison where he died. I showed her where his pictures hung in this house. You can still see the marks if you know where to look. Even when they paint the walls they come through again in a few months. She knows the history of every stone in this house.

MARTHE: Why do you come here every year? There are other places where you could find the sun. You're married, you have money, your own shop. You have a new life.

XENIA: It's natural to want to come back to the place where you were born. Even if it's another world. This house was my home for twenty years. I have friends who've lived on in the town. I like to speak my own language.

MARTHE: Wipe our dust from your feet. That's good advice. This isn't your home anymore. You're a stranger here. Some of the flats have changed hands eight or nine times since you left. Most of the people in them have never heard your family name.

XENIA: The trees in the garden are the same. The lizards must be distant offspring of the ones who were my pets when I was a child. It's the same sea even if it's dirtier. There are still two islands. Some of the cacti I planted on my visits have survived. I came to water them. People put out their cigarette butts in the soil. Lean from the side of their canvas chairs and grind out their cigarettes in it. That's such an ugly thing to do. It desecrates the earth. There's nothing you can say.

ANN *comes in.*

ANN: The third one. I've hung your things in the wardrobe.

XENIA: Bless you. Make a note of the key numbers. I'll telephone Daddy this evening and ask him to send duplicates. We must hope the post delivers them before we go. Don't lose those before you get them back to the hotel.

ANN: Marthe would you like us to go away?

MARTHE: No. Unless staying depresses you.

ANN: It's just that there's nothing we can do to help.

MARTHE: That's not true. Don't be sorry for me. As David can look after me I can stay here to die. I've lived on the sea since I was a child. I'd be unhappy if it was taken away now. David says he can make sure I'll feel no pain.

ANN: What is it like to be told?

XENIA (reproof): Ann.

MARTHE: At first I was sick. Out of fear I suppose. Then I felt it was wrong to give my friends the pain of grieving for me. Well, I've grieved for others and now they'll grieve for me. They'll forgive me. Once when people knew they were dying they prayed and confessed and worried like a dog that had lost its bone. They wasted the little time they had left trying to get a promise they would live for ever. Ridiculous. They could never even know the promise hadn't been given. Death is the most certain of all things yet it's the thing people try to create the most doubt about. When you die you're dead. You don't wake up. There's nothing. This is my last chance of happiness. We all share our lives. If your lives go on in their normal way, so will mine for a little longer. If they don't, I've already started to die. I don't want to do that till I have to. So let's go on as we did before. That's how you can help me.

XENIA: I can't. David says you're dying. That changes everything. I don't know what to do yet – or what to think.

MARTHE: You'll get used to it.

XENIA: You've had six weeks. I'll need more than one day.

ANN: David's taking me out in his boat this afternoon. We'll go for miles and swim in the deep sea. Far out, so that the coast keeps bobbing below the waves. I know you like it there. Come with us.

XENIA: I'd feel as if I were splashing in a puddle.

DAVID comes in.

DAVID: Did they fit?

ANN: Yes.

XENIA: Thank you David.

DAVID: Well that problem's solved. I'll borrow them again for you when you leave. Now you can forget all about it and enjoy your holiday. You're quiet. Have you rowed?

XENIA: You are supposed to be at work.

DAVID: My mother has reticulosis. To be precise a lymphosarcome. The diagnosis is certain but details of the prognosis are not. My mother might live for only a few months from the onset of her illness. A number of new treatments are available here and abroad. A typical example is cis-Platinum. It's given in a drip and causes the patient to vomit for several days. It doesn't appreciably prolong life. I treat my mother with chlorambucil. Doctors have used it for twenty years. Lymphocytes are white blood cells. There's another sort of white blood cell, the polymorphonuclear neutrophils. In lymphosarcome the number of lymphocytes increases greatly, from the normal one to two thousand per cubic millimetre to fifty thousand or even a hundred thousand. As it were, they take over. When such a thing happens the cells circulating in the peripheral blood are no longer mature lymphocytes but immature ones – or even worse, their precursors the lymphoblasts. There's a rush to destruction, as if a nation losing a war had started to put its children into uniform. Then the ravages of death begin. To reduce my mother's WCC – white cell count – I give her each day six milligrammes of chlorambucil. Her total WCC should be between five thousand and fifteen thousand per cubic millimetre. Last week it was twelve thousand five hundred. Now its eleven thousand. Unfortunately chlorambucil also attacks the other white cells, the polymorphonuclear neutrophils, and these are our main protection against infection. That is to say the treatment attacks the body's defences. Yet we must treat. So there is no escape. If necessary death becomes, as it were, an adverse side-affect of the cure. You will have wondered about the manner of my mother's death. Normally cancer patients progressively weaken and waste away. In time they are bedridden. At the end there is coma sometimes complicated with pneumonia. With the reticuloses there is terminally a tendency to exsanguinate. For example from the upper respiratory tract. A nosebleed. As to hope, we might hope that my mother dies sooner and

ANN *leaves the room.*

so more quickly. She has two chances of this. Either by a coronary thrombosis or pulmonary embolism. In coronary thrombosis a coronary artery supplying heart muscle is blocked and the portion of heart muscle normally supplied with blood by that artery dies. If a main coronary artery and consequently a large amount of heart muscle is involved the heart stops immediately. There is collapse, a few sterterous respirations – a sound, we said as students, as of feet struggling to free themselves from quicksand – and then death. My mother is sixty-five. At her age segments of coronary arteries will have been narrowed by plaques of atherome. A tiny haemorrhage in the depths of such plaque would cause it to swell and occlude the artery. Coronary thrombosis follows. The other likely alternative is pulmonary embolism. In pulmonary embolism a clot or thrombus forms in a vein, breaks loose – after which it's known as an embolus – and begins its long floating journey to the right – stage right – atrium of the heart. A few seconds later it blocks a pulmonary artery. If the clot is gross enough death is virtually instantaneous. Marthe's mobility is reduced and she's a bit dehydrated. Together these factors favour the formation of a clot in a leg or the pelvis. This dvt – deep vein thrombosis – may precede pulmonary embolism by hours or days. It announces itself by a swelling of the calf and foot – if a calf vein is involved – or the whole leg if it occurs in a pelvic, iliofemoral vein. As with coronary thrombobis, death is immediate. If my mother were to die in one of these two ways she would to that extent be fortunate. The body

ANN *comes back with a glass of water.*

has not yet evolved means of terminating its life efficiently on all occasions when it's desirable, from the patient's point of view, for it to do so.

ANN *gives* XENIA *the glass.*

XENIA (*to* ANN): Thank you. (*To* DAVID:) How interesting. (*She drinks.*)

Off, a drunk sings.

DAVID: A drunk.

XENIA: From the hotel?

DAVID: Clambering over the rocks. So early. On all fours. Like Father Neptune. Last June one was knocked down in front of the hotel. All fours met four wheels.

XENIA: Ann told me you've invited us to swim with you this afternoon. Thank you, I look forward to it. Excuse me. My cases are open and I can change my clothes.

XENIA *goes.* ANN *sits hunched on the floor down right.* DAVID *goes left, leans on the railings and watches the sea.*

MARTHE: That wasn't necessary.

DAVID: It was necessary for you not her. She will tempt you, Marthe. Don't fall. You are going to die. If I hadn't told you you could pretend. But you know. As long as you are alive you must choose how to live – even though the end's inevitable. You must agree to die. Otherwise you can't die in peace. The time will come when you can't fool yourself. But you won't be prepared. When that happens to someone they die in bitterness. I've seen it. I don't want you to die like that.

MARTHE: Bitterness? I'll be glad to die. I welcome it. 'I lie in bed at night and wait to sleep. I won't know I've died anymore than I know I've fallen asleep.' But why must I wait? There's no happiness left to me now. This isn't my body anymore. Some horrible bundle I carry round. It's coming undone. God knows what will fall out. Give me something, David. Don't make me suffer this. David. David. Let me kill myself. My nose is bleeding.

DAVID (*evenly, without turning round*): That woman's undone everything.

MARTHE: Why is my son cruel?

DAVID (*as before*): When Priam came to Achilles and asked for his murdered son's body Achilles said 'That is the fate gods give wretched men, to suffer while they are free from care'.

MARTHE: Ann, ask him for me. Perhaps he'll do it for you.

ANN *doesn't move.*

DAVID (*as before*): I must go to the garage to buy petrol for the boat. Don't come. There'll be a queue of tourists. The sun and the engines make it as smelly and hot as a furnace.

MARTHE: Shall I wait till you all die? It won't be long before you set fire to yourselves. Your generation will have no memorial. The sound of a whirlwind, the name of a skull. Hiroshima, Nagasaki. People turned into shadows on their doorsteps. Human negatives. The dead living.

DAVID: We'll take a picnic on the boat.

MARTHE (*to herself*): Yak. Human rubbish overflowing from dustbins. Such stench. Dogs mawling it in the gutter. Ha, cry for that!

ANN: I'm not coming.

DAVID (*as before*): We'll leave in an hour. We come back when it's dark. You meet the fishing boats going out and see the men working in the lamp-light on the decks. It would be better if mother took her tablet at the same time each day. I can't always get away from the clinic when I want. You can take charge of her. You'll have to watch her to see she takes them.

ANN *goes.* DAVID *turns, goes to* MARTHE *and offers her tissues.*

MARTHE: I managed on my own.

MARTHE *gets up and goes towards her room.* DAVID *tries to help her.*

Don't touch me. I don't need that help.

DAVID *goes.* MARTHE *goes into her room and shuts the door.*

Three

The house. Afternoon.
MARTHE *sleeps in her chair.* ANN *reads a book.*
DAVID *comes in.*

DAVID (*quietly, to* MARTHE): I'm off to the clinic.

ANN: She's sleeping.

DAVID: Will you be all right on your own?

ANN: I told you I like to be alone sometimes.

DAVID: Yes. I suppose you're busy at home.

ANN: I suppose so. Work, concerts, cinemas. We have a crowd of friends. Daddy brings officers home from his regiment for mother to entertain. Her cooking is famous. In England it's foreign.

DAVID: Why won't you sleep with me any more?

ANN: What can it lead to? I have to go home soon.

DAVID: We were happy last year. When you left you meant to sleep with me. Why've you changed?

ANN: Last year I was a child.

DAVID: Do you have a man friend in England?

ANN: Yes.

DAVID: Do you sleep with him?

ANN: Yes.

DAVID: Is that why you won't sleep with me?

ANN: No.

DAVID: Will you marry this man?

ANN: I don't know.

DAVID: Has he asked you?

ANN: No.

DAVID: What's his name?

ANN: David there's no point in these questions.

DAVID: Sleep with me tonight.

ANN: No.

VOICE (*off, calls*): Ivan.

DAVID: Why not? Is it because mother's dying? Many towns have natal wards and hospices for the dying in the same grounds. Before you knew my mother was dying did you mean to sleep with me?

ANN: No. I made up my mind on the plane.

DAVID: At least the decision was late.

MARTHE (*wakes*): David. What's the time?

DAVID: Twenty past two. I'm late for the

clinic. Are you all right?

MARTHE: Yes.

DAVID (*kisses* MARTHE): Goodbye.

MARTHE: Goodbye.

DAVID *goes.*

MARTHE: Your dress is pretty.

ANN: Mother's boutique. She has good taste.

MARTHE: Is she still in town?

ANN: Yes. She had lunch with a friend.

MARTHE: David looked forward to seeing you. He talked about you a lot – till the last few weeks. Yesterday I remembered something that happened when he was a child. I think of these things because I sit in my chair all day. In winter he wore a thick woolly jumper. He pulled it over his head and thrashed round with his arms and elbows till his head shot through the hole in the top and he shook himself free. I used to be afraid he'd damage his eyes. David can't leave here, Ann. He wouldn't be happy away from the clinic. Would you live here?

ANN: He hasn't asked me. If he did I'd say no. This is mother's house – I know we've been turned out. But that's still how I think of it.

MARTHE: You needn't live in this house.

ANN: I feel as if she was born in the middle ages. What was she like when she was my age?

MARTHE: Very kind. All her family were. They owned half the town. That isn't a figure of speech. Factories, a bank, the local paper, the farms in the hills. Your grandparents were almost royalty. They expected to be bowed at in the streets.

ANN: Were they hated?

MARTHE: Sometimes. They were also loved and respected, which was worse.

ANN: Why?

MARTHE: Some people loved them for what they were, others for what they thought they were. But it didn't matter what they were.

ANN: Why?

MARTHE: When you have so much power you might as well be nobody. Necessity takes over. Industries and banks aren't run by kindness. If they were the world would be much better. After all, we all mean well. Industries and banks run by their own laws. The kindness of one person to another can't change them. Your family made the people who loved and respected them confuse kindness with justice. That is corrupting. You can live without kindness, you can't live without justice – or fighting to get it. If you try to you're mad and don't understand yourself or the world. Then you and everyone else suffer the consequences of your madness. Whole generations bleed for it. The state of injustice is always a state of madness. So what matters isn't what the owners are like or who they are. They must never be the chosen few – even if they are the best – but the many.

ANN: You're severe.

MARTHE: Some things require such severity.

XENIA *comes in.*

XENIA: How are you?

MARTHE: Fine.

ANN: Did you enjoy your visit?

XENIA (*produces a bottle*): Look, brandy from the duty free shop. Not local fire water. I've already had a tot. Are you allowed to drink some?

MARTHE: Yes, please.

XENIA: You're sure? I don't want to be arraigned by the medical authorities.

ANN: I'll get some glasses.

ANN *goes.*

XENIA: My visit wore me out. I sat and listened to three hours of complaints. What can I do? I'm helpless. The neighbours' children are noisy. I shouted at them. They ran away laughing. After fifteen minutes they came back and were even noisier. She has no friends. No one calls. All the people she knew are dead or abroad. Every morning she gets up and brushes her hair into that bun she's worn for fifty years – and it's been grey for twenty.

ANN *comes back with three glasses.*

Then she sits in a chair till the light in its mercy fades and she can creep across her room to bed. You serve. (ANN *pours*.) It upset me. To go on living after the world's been taken away from you. (ANN *gives her a glass*.) Thank you. Cheers. (*She drinks*.) A disgraceful neglect of an old woman.

MARTHE: I'll ask David to call on her.

XENIA: She doesn't need a doctor. She's as tough as a horse or she wouldn't have survived. She needs companionship.

MARTHE: I know. I used to call on her. It became too tiring. She hates so many things. She's thrown her life away.

XENIA: Oh, I did some shopping. (*From a bag*.) There.

MARTHE: What is it?

XENIA: A waiter's crumb brush.

MARTHE: For me?

XENIA: The birds. You throw them your crumbs. Now you can do it in comfort and not waste any. I hope they sing louder. My grandmother gave them as Christmas presents.

ANN: Where did you get it?

XENIA: The old ironmongers. They had a box of them in the back of the storeroom. If you make a fuss they'll find anything. (*She sips*.) This is good. When I was a girl we went to the islands almost every day in the summer. Often we camped there. Mother and father would bring their friends for the day. There was always some young man who could play the mandolin. The women sat under silk sunshades and the men rolled up their trouser-legs and stood in the shallows to fish. I expected an old Chinaman to come out of a cave and kneel to pray or draw a map of the sky in the sand. At night we dived from the rocks and floated in the sea and looked at the stars. I'm sorry. Seeing the old woman upset me. She was my father's friend. She came here to our dinners. After the grown-ups had eaten they sat out here on the terrace. If I was a good child I was allowed to sit with them. The family and the guests talked quietly as if they were in awe of the moon, it was so high. On this terrace. And down in the garden. It was a garden then. Often a breeze came off the sea and blew the scents of the flowers and shrubs over us. I sat in my father's lap and listened to his

heart and the racing of his watch. He bought his cigars in Paris. Then the farmers sang in the hills. I expect my father paid for their songs. We listened in silence. The farmers worked hard and yet they created that beauty. I fell asleep on my father's lap and woke in my bed. In those days my happiness frightened me – it was so great I thought I would die of it. Long ago. I didn't know that men who sang so beautifully could hate so deeply. I still don't believe it. That's how we lived till the fanatics came. Then the crowds cheered and waved and marched as if the town had been taken over by a circus. And after them came the war. Shells. Sea mines. Foreign uniforms. The ugly little huts on the islands. People hounded and tortured and shot. And when the war was over they threw down the gods and goddesses from the terraces. Zeus, Hera and Aphrodite lay on the rocks with no arms or heads. Our fault. It has all gone. We were foolish. It will never be given back. I hope those who have it are happy. What's the use of saying all this?

ANN: More?

XENIA: A drop. (ANN *pours*.) Thank you.

MARTHE: I want to tell Ann something.

XENIA: Oh dear, now I've upset Marthe. How silly of me to rake up the past. How stupid.

MARTHE: You know that once I was going to be shot.

ANN: Shot? No! By us?

MARTHE: Haven't you told her?

XENIA (*shrugs*): There seemed no point. (*She sips*.) This is good.

MARTHE: It was the Germans. A German soldier on a motor-bike was shot at. The motor-bike crashed and both the driver and an officer in the sidecar were killed. The Germans took hostages. Two hundred for the officer and a hundred for the driver. In those days when you saw Germans you hid or hurried away. I was trapped in a sidestreet and taken to the islands.

ANN: These islands?

MARTHE: Yes. Your family still owned them then.

XENIA: It was terrible. The Germans commandeered them for a concentration camp. They insisted on paying rent.

MARTHE: Your mother persuaded the German commandant to let me go.

ANN: You saved Marthe's life! Why have you never told me?

XENIA: What was there to tell? We all helped each other under the occupation. I wanted to save them all but I could only ask for Marthe: she was our servant. The commandant probably thought that if his soldiers shot her it would make conversation awkward the next time he came to dinner. He shot the others. We were used to shooting by then. They shot people every day on the islands. For months on end. You could hear it on this terrace. The irony was that father passed information to the partisans through Marthe. That's why we had the Germans to dine. They trusted us and we overheard many things that helped the partisans. You see what a brave grandfather you had. If the Germans had found out they'd have shot him and his family. Not that it helped him after the war.

MARTHE: We were shut in a hut for a day and a half. The barred window had been boarded with planks. Most of us sat on a wooden bench that ran round the inside of the hut. There wasn't room on it for everyone. Some sat on the floor in the middle. We were all women. The men and children were in other huts.

ANN: Children?

MARTHE: The Germans began to shoot the men. We heard bursts of firing. I don't know why we didn't go mad. People seem to be able to bear almost anything. A few prayed. Some cried. Others cursed. No one turned to the wall. We looked at each other. Of course I'd known that I might be shot. But I didn't know how to die. What you did at the end.

XENIA: That's enough. (*She sips.*)

MARTHE: When a German was shot everything was taken. Papers, uniform, boots, weapons – everything that could be used. Once – after I'd been released – I found a wallet on one of them. Inside there was a photograph of his father and mother. Then one of his girl. And at the

back two of the war. One of these showed six or seven naked women standing in a group in a field. The print was blurred. Wartime chemicals. You couldn't see where they were. There were some trees in the distance and a dark shape that might have been a barn. At one side a grey figure pointed a rifle at them. Very neat and trim. I think his boots were polished. A toy soldier. He must have had other soldiers with him but you couldn't see them. The other photograph also showed women. Two neighbours or a mother and daughter. They were bundled up in clothes and their heads were hidden in scarves. They turned away so that their heads were in shadow. The place was misty or perhaps the film was bad. Wartime quality. If it wasn't for the little hill under their feet they might have been in the clouds. There were no soldiers in this picture. Nothing to show the women were going to be shot. But I knew they were. Immediately. From the gesture of their head and shoulders. It was the gesture of the first photograph. They huddled together and turned away as if it had started to rain. That was how you died. Simply. As if you walked out of life. I knew some of the women with me in the hut by sight. I'd seen them in town. One woman began to tell us about her life. She'd married an elderly farmer. Her son had been killed in the war. She'd come down to town to sell his clothes and been rounded up. We took turns to say who we were and how we'd lived. We gave our names to pass on if any of us survived. It was as if we were in a schoolroom and were going to die. There was an old woman beside me on the bench. She was so doubled over that if she died facing the soldiers the bullets went in her back. She'd lost everything – her family and her room. When I told them the name of the woman I worked for she said 'If I could live to spit in her face' and spat in the dirt. Later a soldier came in. Most of the women ran to the other end of the hut and wailed. The soldier shouted my name over the noise. I followed him out. While he chained the door he turned to grin at me. He made the thumbs up sign as if I'd won a lottery. He led me along the side of the hut. You were standing beside an officer. You held the strap of your patent leather handbag in both hands. The soldier saluted. You nodded.

XENIA: To identify you.

MARTHE: The officer clicked and saluted you. I followed you to the landing place and onto the military boat.

XENIA: It was windy and choppy. We didn't say anything. If you'd thanked me I'd have laughed.

MARTHE: I spent the next day in my room. I heard the shooting from there. Two hours. I wondered what batch I'd have been in. Several times I thought it was over but it started again.

XENIA: After the war the guards on the island were changed. My father was arrested as an exploiter. Perhaps they put him in Marthe's hut. He was sentenced to ten years hard labour. He escaped by dying in two. My mother had already died during the war. When father was arrested friends took me in. I was smuggled out of the country in an army lorry. That's how I met your father. (*She sips.*) Some of those who arrested him were among those he'd passed information to. What happened as they left the house became a legend in our family. A servant opened the door and my father said 'Thank you'. One of his captors said 'Let him learn to open doors' and another said 'His door will be locked'. They led him away through the garden. There should have been fruit on the trees. A crowd had picked it early. They were too hungry to notice they ate sour fruit. (*She sips.*) I can't understand why you punished him. I understand why you took his house, money, clothes, cattle, land, books, pictures, umbrella – but why punish him? He was an old man who wasn't used to manual work. It was a sentence of death. He had faults. A bad temper. He once hit my mother. But he didn't choose the bed he was born in. He behaved as they all did in his position. Someone must run the world. If you do it better, fine. But why punish him? Nothing was too petty for his trial. Each time he swore at a taxi driver or dismissed someone for bad time-keeping. It was all remembered. They forgave him nothing. Even you gave evidence against him.

MARTHE: I described how he lived. The parties and gambling. Many in the court had starved. It was dangerous to live in your father's world.

ANN: Don't quarrel. Let me think about what you've both told me.

XENIA: Yes, think. And learn what people do in this world. Once those islands were one piece of rock. Then the sea tore them in two. I've seen men and women who could have torn them apart with their bare hands their hatred was so great. How can you sit and look at them all day?

MARTHE: I've lived a second life for forty years. Now I've come to my second death. It's a beautiful summer. The very old people say it's the best they remember. I'm lucky but I can't hope to live nine lives. The islands change colour all the time. In the evening they're dark. They're called the eyes of the sea. Why should I mind them? They're not my life. This house is my life. My mother was its first housekeeper and I would have been its second. I came here as a servant. Now I live here by right. I could have died on that island. I was saved – not even by a friend but by an enemy. That's how lucky I was! When the house was made into flats people said I should be caretaker. I went on the town council and served there till this summer. We built a clinic and a school and houses. Now I sit on the terrace and watch the sea. During the day as the shadow moves over the stones I move my chair to stay in the sun. When David was studying he put his table in front of his window where the sun fell on it. As it moved he moved his chair so that he read and made his notes in the sun. When I mind my neighbour's children I put them on the floor and they crawl to the sun. They cry at the dark but no one cries at the light. That's what I've learned. I have no memory of the islands to drive me out of the sun to cry in my cave.

XENIA: You're right. Don't be frightened of bogeymen. (*To* ANN, *refusing a drink.*) No, it's too early. I haven't been on the island for years. Ask David to take us in his boat.

VOICE (*off, calls*): Ivan.

ANN: Who's Ivan?

XENIA: All the men here are called Ivan.

MARTHE: Two girls arm in arm are calling a young man in a rowing boat.

VOICE (*off, calls*): Ivan.

ANN: Has he heard?

MARTHE: Yes. They're waving to each other. When we were young parents took their new babies down to the rocks on a sunny day, held them over their heads and shouted their names to the sea. It was a custom.

Four

The island. A sandy floor before a rock wall.
XENIA *sits alone.*
A GERMAN *comes on.*

GERMAN: Speak German?

XENIA: Yes.

GERMAN: Good. Your boat is tied up at the mooring. Please take me back to the hotel.

XENIA: Is your boat lost?

GERMAN: My son and daughter-in-law dropped me on the island and went for a trip along the coast. They should have been back two hours ago. I can't see their boat on the water. They've made me late for the evening meal. When you take the pension with full board you must come to the restaurant for the evening meal by eight-thirty. It is better to be there at seven-thirty. Then there is time to ask for seconds.

XENIA: Your son and daughter-in-law will come back. They'll worry if you're not here.

GERMAN: That will teach them to make their elders wait. If I'm late I won't be served with the evening meal. The waiters are stern with those who come late. They want to go home.

XENIA: My friend will take you in his boat. Wait at the landing. No, sit in the boat under the awning.

GERMAN: Have they left you on your own? Our young people! I don't complain. Sigi could not be a more dutiful son. His Haidi is like my daughter. Since my wife died I would be lonely without them. They take me on holiday every year. I haven't seen you at the hotel.

XENIA: I stay with friends.

GERMAN: Oh, friends are better than a hotel. The young people are not married?

XENIA: No.

GERMAN: I see them often. The other day I saw them on the rocks. The young man talked to the girl and tried to press himself on her. Our young people!

XENIA: If you care to wait in the boat.

GERMAN: Oh, I said something to shock. You have no reason to complain about the young lady. That is a good daughter. She pushed the young man away.

XENIA: Thank you. I would like to be on my –

GERMAN: You are right. It's wrong for the elders to tell the young people what to do. Sometimes they set us a good example. They remind us we're still young and on holiday! I saw them just now from the mouth of the ammunition cave. They went down the other side of the island. You can't see so far from the cave. If you are concerned for the young lady I shall wander down and pretend to look for something I have lost.

XENIA: You were here in the war.

GERMAN: Ja. I said ammunition cave. That gave me away. You know what happened here in the war?

XENIA: Yes, I lived here.

GERMAN: Ah, that war. Terrible. Terrible. Terrible. So much killing. (*He calls:*) Sigi! Haidi! (*To* XENIA:) Haidi is a sensible girl and Sigi has a good underwater watch. But they lose all sense of time. They didn't go off to enjoy themselves without me. They think I want to be on my own for a while. It's their way to be kind. It would have been good to come back with comrades and talk of the old days. These islands were a camp. Prisoners were routed on. Terrible times. Tcha. But we must make the best of it. Even in the end – till the very last days – we went to the bars in the evenings to drink a glass of wine and sing the old songs. I carried my accordion all through the war till I got back to Germany. I had to barter it for food. Ruins and blackmarket, that's all that was left. There was no music in my life for years. But we recovered. The spirit inside was not broken. That is what counts. You have a grudge against us?

XENIA: You destroyed our lives.

GERMAN: No no, the old days were over. No one was strong enough to save them. Now we must learn to live in a new world. When I got back all my people were dead. The elders, aunts, my brother, even my girl. My family took her in when she was bombed out. They all died together in one house. After the war I married her sister. I have a good job. I sell refrigerators. I can give you a discount. You could bring it over the border.

XENIA: I live in England.

GERMAN: Ah, you married an Englander? It is sad not to live in your own country. I'll tell you a secret. Do you know where we are? Guess. This spot. That was the execution wall.

XENIA: Oh.

GERMAN: In Germany we would put a statue there. We have many artists. When prisoners were shot the lizards jumped into the cracks and stayed there till we left. Then they came out to sit in the sun. You have something to eat in your bag?

XENIA: Yes.

GERMAN: There are butter marks on the paper. Today we had lunch early so the children could have full use of the boat. You must hire one for the day. Not cheap. If you don't eat here the sun makes you ill. I learned that from the war.

XENIA (*food*): Please eat this. It's left from our lunch.

GERMAN: Ah, sandwich. How English. (*He eats.*) Good. Thank you. It is better to be kind than make terrible wars. But it had to be.

XENIA: Were you here long?

GERMAN: For the duration. There's nothing to hide. We were questioned after the war. By GI Jonny. This wasn't a concentration camp. We were private soldiers: not officers, not Gestapo, not guilty. We garrisoned the town, guarded the roads, kept the prisoners. When we took them to be questioned we handed them over at the door. It had to be. The civvies killed us and our officers. Not in fair play you understand. They crept up on our sentries at night and cut their throats with a knife. People who do these things must be dealt with. Poor bastards. I was sorry for them. I did nothing they wouldn't have done to me. Crumbs fall into your hair when you eat sandwiches naked. (*He laughs and brushes crumbs from his chest.*)

XENIA: You didn't kill anyone.

GERMAN: Oh, yes. Sometimes. When it was urgent. It was forbidden to be questioned or killed on this island. Prisoners were taken to the little island first. To begin with regulations were strictly enforced. But what can you do when prisoners are sitting in the boats and there is no petrol for the engines? You can row them across but it's hard. There are so many prisoners. So organisation broke down and discipline became lax: we knew the end was coming. We started to shoot prisoners here. There was such disorganisation it could even happen that ammunition ran out. Headquarters gave the order: hostages. There is no alternative. It is easy to say hostages, it's not so easy to say ammunition. Many times our CO had to go on the scrounge. He was called a scrounger as if he cadged cigarettes. No, he was a generous man. But the officers fell out and swore at each other. Not the behaviour of gentlemen. Bad blood between comrades. The batmen and clerks told us everything. Commander Lauber said: 'If you want to play the hero and get a medal for shooting people use your own ammunition'. That's how things were. How could we win a war like that? They tried to sink them in ships. But we ran out of ships. The fishermen sank theirs before we could get them. We needed ours to patrol the coast. So that was called off. Yes, it's good to remember how hard things were. At one time many people were buried on this island. They were killed here so where could we put them? In a war bodies are a problem even to Germans. Take them to the mainland? More work, more porters, boats, more lorries to take them from the quay to the hills. Throw them into the sea? No tide. The beaches are fouled. The town can't go about its business. You would think this was the devil's island it was so difficult for our adjutant to run. Now I will tell you about the end. When we had to go home. By then the island was full of bodies. They had been sealed up in caves and pushed down cracks. The soldiers said if the island was a coat the pockets would bulge! The order came: exhume the dead and throw them into the sea. We were angry. It would seem as if we had something to hide. Our enemies were quick to lie about us. We were not criminals. We'd done everything in the open. According to laws of war. Harsh – but war is harsh. Now we must open the graves. Dig the bodies out of the rocks. It is an order. We stood guard while the prisoners dug and carried. Such stench. Can you imagine? For three days. The bodies were thrown into the sea. But there is no tide. The bodies won't go away. The sea will not take them. It is as if it was against us. They floated round the island. Only a few were skeletons. Sand had preserved the skin of the rest. They drifted on the surface or just below it. Some of them held hands – that's how they died. When we went to the land for supplies – Oh the evenings of songs in the bars were over by then – our boats towed the bodies behind us in our wakes as if they were swimming after us and pointing at us with their outstretched hands – that's how they died. A dead woman clutched a child in the crook of her arm and floated on top of the sea as if she held the child up out of the water to see us. The public address system played dance music to keep spirits high. We came with marches and left with waltzes. (*He looks round.*) Where are those bad children? I was lucky to find someone to speak German. This is my first time in your country since the war. Haidi and Sigi brought me here as a surprise. Other years we went to Majorca. Malta. Spain. Italy twice. Majorca six times. Majorca is best for a holiday. The Crusader Hotel is excellent. Reasonable terms. So is the hotel here. And it's new. It works. Next year nothing will work. Yes, I remember those days well. We cut our initials and army numbers in the rock. Now they're gone. The wind erases them with a handful of sand. But it couldn't have done it so soon. It's not so strong. Hooligans did it. And put their initials in our place. You are quiet, madam. Is it the sun? Have I eaten your food? I think my stories upset you. This was not one of the bad camps. In the bad camps people were burned. Some of their guards collapsed with fatigue. They were transferred to us here. This was a good posting by the sea. They said that in those places so much fat hung in the air you covered your coffee with your hand and drank from beneath it. It even got into their skin so they didn't smell of themselves anymore. They smelt of other people. Or like the dead. When they were on leave their wives thought they were in bed with a stranger. Ho hoo! That's an army for you! Take the clothes off your back and put you in uniform. Take your name and give you a number. Take your head and stuff it with orders. Then take your skin – and you end up smelling of someone else. Is that bread? (*He points.*) Talking is good for the appetite. I mustn't be greedy. Even if Sigi came now we'd be late for the restaurant. If we go there one minute late they turn us away. The young ones spoil me. I can have what I want at the bar. I say no, such extravagance is a waste. Why pay for food you don't eat? Between us we'd lose three meals. The hotel doesn't lose. Tomorrow the kitchen serves our steaks as casserole.

XENIA (*food*): Please take it.

GERMAN (*eating*): Good. Thank you. Crept up on our sentries with a knife. Slick.

XENIA: We killed as many of you as we could.

GERMAN: Of course, of course. Natural after the rumours that spread about us. People like to believe the worst.

XENIA: I know what happened. (*She points.*) I lived over there.

GERMAN (*laughs*): We were that close? I sailed under those cliffs many times. You see that big house? Our officers dined there. In the war there was a young girl, the daughter of the house. We called her the girl in white. She stood on the terrace and pretended to stare at the sea. Hour after hour for days at a time. We sang to her as we sailed below or swam. We watched her through binoculars. Our comrades throats were cut. They said it was quieter than shooting – but that's how they liked to do it. We loved her, we were young soldiers. She never smiled or waved. She dared not. The partisans would have shot her. But she was our friend. She stood there as a sign. It was all she could do.

XENIA: I don't understand!

GERMAN: We didn't come here as enemies. We were defenders. Could we have done all we did out of hate? No, our officers said: we acted in honour. To save you from scum.

XENIA: What nonsense!

GERMAN: You see! Our officers were right: all that blood and suffering and nothing is learned. Europe was threatened. Civilization, Beethoven, art. What else is there? Americans and pygmies.

XENIA: She didn't stand there for your sake! I expect she was lonely! So many young men were killed! She wondered how long she had to live.

GERMAN: Men are animals. We can't be trusted with another man's wife or his money. Not even with our own daughters. No one's safe on our streets at night. If we don't get our fodder we whine. What saves us from ourselves? Culture. The standards of our fathers. They struggled for centuries to make them strong. But standards are always as weak as the girl in white. Always. The animal wants to be on top. If that happens we're lost. The apes come out of their jungle. That's why we went to war.

XENIA: You're talking nonsense!

GERMAN: The girl in white could tell you!

XENIA: You invade us, bomb us, rob us – for our good!

GERMAN: That was because you listened to scum. If we'd listened to scum Europe would be a labour camp. If you'd helped us there'd be more hope for the world. Instead you'll see what happens. The jungles are open.

XENIA: Go away.

GERMAN: I can show you the truth. There was a woman who worked for the girl on the balcony. Servant. She was taken hostage: more throats had been cut. The girl asked our commander to let her go. Now parents had begged us for their children on the streets. Tried to climb on the lorries to take their place. We pushed them off. But our commander gave that servant back to the girl. We weren't angry for our dead comrades. Some of us had tears in our eyes. That girl had a right to ask us for anything. We were at war for her. What happens to our culture, our way of life, when people like that go? She

came from the same class as our officers. She knew that – and what it meant. It was proved when she came and asked for the woman. She needn't have asked, she could have given an order! I wish I could meet her and thank her for all she did for us. It was not to be. When we left her class were shot or chased out. They put some of them in our old huts.

XENIA: How dare you! Who are you? Who told you to say these things to me? Someone paid you!

GERMAN: Ah, you're one of those who benefited from the pickings. You did well out of the end of the war so you see it from that point of view.

XENIA (picks up her bag): Go away!

GERMAN: Oh, madam, don't be angry. Thank you for the sandwich. The heat. My empty stomach. I rambled on. Yes, but I will not be humiliated even if I stay on this island all night – at my age that would not be easy. I came here in my prime. I risked my life. The sacrifice of young manhood should be respected. Our young people would have to do all we did if those times come again. It would have to be.

XENIA: Wait here. My daughter's friend will take you in his boat.

GERMAN: It's better if I wait on board. You said under the shade.

XENIA: Don't follow me!

GERMAN: Your friend will leave in a hurry without me.

XENIA: Stop following me! I shall report you to the police!

XENIA goes.

GERMAN (shouting after her): My dear lady, I didn't touch you! Oh dear, Sigi and Haidi are drowned! (He starts to follow XENIA.) Haidi wouldn't let him be rash –

XENIA (off): Go away!

GERMAN: – but he doesn't know these waters. The rocks are dangerous. It would be terrible to go home alone.

The GERMAN goes. ANN and DAVID come on.

DAVID: This island is sacred to us. I won't make love to another girl here. Why am I so happy? From now on we have a secret power: whenever we're angry or sad we'll think of this and it will make us happy. We have fallen in love. Perhaps you will not stay here. Then instead I shall plant a pine in the place where we were today. I'll water it till it grows tall and strong. I'll scatter seed under it so that flocks of birds come there to live. This is the wall where my mother was to be shot. Look at the fossils and veins of quartz and bullet marks in the rock. When they shot simple people – not fighters or hardened politicians but children and old women – they dragged the dead out of sight so that the simple people wouldn't know where they were and run away. There was blood on the ground – but there was blood on all the rocks on the island and on the walls of the rooms. So they thought there was still time for a plane to come out of the sky, or a hand – or a friendly boat to appear on the sea. That was at the start of the war. After a time they made even the simple people climb over the bodies to the wall. If they stumbled they clubbed them. The Assyrian has said I will make him more dead than he was before. The Spaniard has said I will kill the dead twice.

The GERMAN *comes in.*

GERMAN: Speak German?

DAVID: Yes.

GERMAN: Thank god. That is your boat, sir. Goodday, miss. Please take me to the hotel.

DAVID: Are you stranded?

GERMAN: Sigi hired a boat to surprise Haidi. Now they're lost. I must get back for the evening meal. The door of the restaurant is shut at eight-thirty sharp. If you tap on the glass the waiters look away and the guests hold up the food on their forks and laugh. You can't get the manager, he's cleaning the pool.

DAVID: You can come with us.

GERMAN: Thank you, thank you. I sweat with anxiety. You must not let the lady attack me. I didn't touch her. Sigi and Haidi will be cross. The lady in Ibiza had too much sun oil on her leg. The sand set in the crease. I brushed it off. I don't want any scandal. Because I'm German the older generation – it's natural.

DAVID: I'll take you in my boat.

GERMAN: We work for our holiday. You too. A song in the evening and a glass of wine. I wanted it all to go well today. Three weeks pass so quickly. Tomorrow we go back to Bächelstein. Tonight I wanted to buy a special bottle of wine. Yesterday was Sigi and Haidi's turn. That's how we end our holidays. A toast to the next year.

DAVID: Don't be distressed. Wait in the boat.

GERMAN: The lady is angry. I'll wait on the path. Not to go to the boat till you come? When you pass me on the way down I'll follow you. The lady must not say such things. I don't molest ladies.

DAVID: Ann. Death creates desire. Lust. The stupid think that's perverse. No. Lust isn't drawn to death. When life sees death it becomes strong itself, it *will* be strong. While we cry our distorted mouth reaches for one that smiles. We'll sleep together every night till you go away. I will plant a great treasure of seed in you to carry abroad to your country. There you will bear a child. The child and that pine are the only things we can give to my mother – or all who die.

ANN: A tense woman sitting upright in a corner of a boat. A hungry old man squatting in the dust halfway down to the landing place. They each have their own thoughts. Angry, offended, waiting for planes, suspecting waiters, staring at their watches. The stranger should be grateful he met us. My mother is angry because we made her wait while we went to the other side of the island. I don't wish to make her angry but it doesn't matter if she is. 'The gods love the widespread races of happy man and willingly lengthen the days of his fleeting life, to share with him the joyful view from their unchanging sky, for a brief span of time.' They're on the edge of the island waiting to leave. We're free and told to be happy. Let's sit here a little longer.

Five

The house. Night.
Empty.
XENIA *comes on. She taps on* MARTHE's *door.*

XENIA: Can I speak to you? (*Slight pause.*) You're not asleep. I looked into your room from the garden.

XENIA *walks away from the door. After a moment* MARTHE *comes out.*

MARTHE: Yes?

XENIA: I must speak to you.

MARTHE: Can't it wait till morning? (*No answer.*) Move my chair. There's a breeze.

XENIA *puts* MARTHE'*s chair stage centre.* MARTHE *sits in it.*

XENIA: David and Ann are out.

MARTHE: Dancing at the hotel. Does it shock you?

XENIA: It's not my concern. No doubt he wouldn't dance if he thought you cared. Shall I come here when you're dead?

MARTHE: That doesn't concern me.

XENIA: I'll do what you want.

MARTHE: Live your own life.

XENIA: You might wish me to come. I'd keep your memory alive: I knew you so well.

MARTHE: Do as you please.

XENIA: Have I ever shown you any resentment?

MARTHE: I'm tired now.

XENIA: I was an only child. When my father died this house – all he had – would have been mine. It was taken from me even before he died. Some of the people who took it had been with us for years. Your son thinks if I was here he'd be blacking boots. It shows even when he smiles. My father sent clever children to the university whatever their background. Paid their tuition fees, bought their books, clothed some of them, gave them an allowance –

MARTHE: What d'you want to say?

XENIA: – but I've never held a grudge.

MARTHE: No.

XENIA: Then why do you despise me?

MARTHE: I don't.

XENIA: So does your son. Only he's more offensive because he has no excuse. I'm tired of being abused and attacked.

MARTHE: If you have a complaint about David make it to him. I'm sorry if he's been rude to you. He's young and thoughtless.

XENIA: He thinks I want to come back here. I knew that life couldn't go on. I was hated and resented even when I was a small child. If I'd had to spend my life like that I'd be old and embittered now. Instead I have a good husband, my daughter and kind friends. There's my shop. I sell the best clothes as cheaply as I can and have the pleasure of seeing nice young people enjoying life. At their age we could have been shot. Many of our friends were. D'you seriously think I want to go back to all that? Life has been good to me. And there's nothing I need blame myself for. Whatever my family did, Marthe, I was young when I left – for *those* days little more than a child. Yet you despise me.

MARTHE: No.

XENIA: Don't you know you do? Your condition's worse than I thought. It's a disease you don't even know you've got. That's why you've passed it on to your son. Has he got to live with it after you're dead? D'you want to ruin his life? Can't we get rid of the past even now? Let's sit here quietly till he comes and then the three of us will talk.

MARTHE: What about?

XENIA: Oh Marthe, you wrong yourself! You know. My daughter told you how much I keep secret. I never tell her things that would shame anyone she knew. But if this is to be your last summer, then at least we two should be honest with each other. I saved your life. Yet you gave evidence against us. Not out of fear. You weren't forced. My father might have been shot. How wrong. Such guilt is almost unforgiveable.

MARTHE: What guilt? Let us talk about ourselves. People in my generation had to depend on your family in order to live. But why should that have been? Your kindness made us beggars. It made some of us grateful, which was worse. There can never be enough kindness to make the world human. If you spent your life being kind people would still die of neglect and ignorance. Much more is needed. Let's leave it till the morning. Years ago your father's bank was robbed and a girl cashier shot. The man who did it hid on the island. Your father saw him through his binoculars and went out in his motor-boat. A group of men were standing beside him at the wheel. The young man saw them and realised he'd been discovered. He jumped into the water and swam for the shore. Your father chased him. He turned and swam towards the open sea. He was that desperate. When your father's men dragged him on board he struggled like a madman to get back in the water. They had to tie him up and lay him on the bottom of the boat as if he was a corpse. Did your father rescue him from drowning or catch a fish for dinner? While that went on your mother and her ladies took tea on the terrace. They weren't a vulgar mob, they didn't line the railings to cheer. They quietly drank their tea. If your father had brought the man here your mother would have given him tea and wrapped him in her stole. Would that have made his punishment easier to bear? The foundations of your world were crooked and so everything in it was crooked. Kindness, consideration, consistency were meaningless. All the good you did was meaningless. In your world the good did evil. What could be worse? Most of us spent our lives swimming towards the open sea. The soldiers on the island didn't have much excuse for not seeing the blood they shed. You were worse, you had every excuse for what you did. Your world was a puppet show and you thought the puppets moved because of the little bits of wood under their bright coats – not the strings. Banks, factories, shops, governments – these things control our lives. What we are depends on the relationship between us and them. Faced with that kindness is like blowing on a storm to make it go away. But when those relationships are just we will live justly. Kindness will have its meaning. Justice and mercy will be one.

XENIA: You remember what you choose! My father was a liberal man. When that thief was sentenced to death my father used his newspaper to get him reprieved. The dead girl's family came here to abuse him. I had to be taken out for a walk so I didn't hear the vile things they said. The fascists demonstrated. Their party membership doubled. Father resisted them. We were happy when that man was saved!

MARTHE: I can't say anymore. Your father was as kind as you. He could afford it. His money shone not his halo. The young man was so grateful to your father that when the war came he volunteered and was shot. People like you seem to live backwards. You spend your lives burrowing through the ground to your grave. Well, you have no more power. That's what matters.

XENIA: Now you admit you despise me.

MARTHE: How do you live through the last moments? The last hour in hospital. Walking out of the cell. Perhaps I should have stayed in the hut when you came. I could have helped the others. Put my arms round the old women or helped the girls who stumbled. I might even have sung. I wanted to fly into the line of light under the door. Then the door opened. I'd secretly begged for life. Not hoped, calculated. I knew you'd come. I left them to die alone – as I am now. I should have stayed. They're dead, the huts are burned, the island's free. It hasn't changed for me. I saw a photograph of my death. I lived my second life in another way. I listen to them not you.

XENIA: You shouldn't. They're dead and you're not. When I was a student you were a servant. I envied you. You had more dignity, more intelligence, than the rest of us. Now our roles are reversed. I got away – but you're corrupted by the past.

XENIA *goes. Music starts in the distance.* MARTHE *doesn't react.* XENIA *returns.*

The discotheque. Now I shan't sleep.

MARTHE: It stops after midnight.

XENIA: I'd better take you to your room.

MARTHE: I'm all right.

XENIA: I shan't come here again. My husband told me not to. This is my grave. They say in prison my father's hair turned white in a week. I didn't see him. I should have drowned myself when they took him away. Gone down the rocks in the dark and slipped into the sea. Now it's too late. They'd say 'A bitter old woman'. I'm not.

It's just that you took everything from me – and still want more!

MARTHE: What could I want? Go to your room. It's quieter on your side of the house. I spent so much of my life in struggle. Lost so many friends. New clothes become old when I put them on. I'm worn out. I listen to the air going in and out of my body. Like footsteps in a corridor. It's not easy: it's as if a crowd had to die.

XENIA: The world was taken away from me. They threw the furniture out of the house and left me in the emptiness. I can't begin again. I've spent years pointing at my dead body – and no one sees it.

MARTHE: Yes, you can't begin. You belong to a family who die in prisons. The old woman beside me. Gripped the bench with both hands. Her knuckles shone like a child's. 'If I could live to spit in her face.' (MARTHE *heaves herself half out of her chair, spits in* XENIA'*s face and falls back again on the floor.*) It's gone.

XENIA: How dare you! Because you're dying you think you can be a monster! Oh you must feel better! You carried a dead woman's spit round in your mouth for forty years! I shan't sleep here. I'll go to the hotel. Send my things on in the morning. I won't trouble you to give a message to my daughter. I'll write a note.

XENIA *goes.* MARTHE *doesn't move.* XENIA *returns.*

Are you all right? If you wish I'll help you to your room.

MARTHE: Go away.

XENIA: It's clear you're not well. The drugs you take have affected you. I don't want to be accused of letting you die of exposure. No doubt your son would give evidence against me.

XENIA *goes to* MARTHE.

MARTHE: Get out.

XENIA: As you wish. I'll leave you to suffer the consequences of your stubborness.

XENIA *goes.* MARTHE *stands, goes to her room and tries the handle of the door. She can't turn it. For a moment she rests on the wall. She tries the handle again. The door opens.* MARTHE *goes into her room and shuts the door behind her.*

Six

The house. Morning.
A trestle table down right. MARTHE *lays breakfast.*
ANN *comes in.*

ANN: Good morning.

MARTHE: Good morning. How are you?

ANN: Fine. And you? I have mother's note. You two have quarrelled.

MARTHE: It's nothing.

ANN: What was it about?

MARTHE: It's finished.

ANN: Really, you behave like children. Mother is difficult but she wouldn't leave without a reason.

MARTHE: Please ask her.

ANN: Oh, Marthe! (*She sighs.*) I suppose you're upset. Was it about David and me?

MARTHE: I made this jam. A neighbour gave me some plums from her tree. The big woman. You've seen her child playing with her apron while she hangs out her washing.

ANN: I'll lay the table.

MARTHE: I'll do it.

ANN: It's so much nonsense. You make me cross. Are you quarrelling with me now?

MARTHE: Don't be rude. Laying the table is one of the few jobs I can still do. I covered the table with a clean cloth and brought a pot of petunias from the roof. Hand me the plates. (*They lay the table together.*) Was there a storm last night?

ANN: No.

MARTHE: I dreamed I went to sleep and in the night a door banged in the wind. I woke up and listened to the sea. I must have been sleeping all the time. This morning everything looks as if it had been in a storm. Dust and bits of paper and rubbish blown away. Boxes and tins blown to the sides of the houses. The leaves are still crooked from the wind. The town looks as battered and new as a child that's cried itself to sleep.

ANN: There wasn't a storm.

MARTHE: No, I dreamed it. Give me the knives.

MARTHE *lays the table.*

I'll set a place for your mother. I don't think she'll come, but she might and it would be better if she found a place set for her. Perhaps she'll come to breakfast tomorrow. Or perhaps she won't. Fetch the coffee and milk from the kitchen. The petunia needs water.

ANN: I'm hungry.

MARTHE: Wait for David.

ANN: He's asleep.

MARTHE: Wake him. Is he a good lover?

ANN: Yes.

MARTHE: The three of us will eat together. I'll cut the bread.

ANN: Marthe. Your ankle's swollen.

MARTHE: It began in the night. I found it like that this morning.

ANN: It must hurt.

MARTHE: No. I stood on it too long. I'll rest it later. Don't tell David. He'll give me more tablets. Pass my wrap. (ANN *gives* MARTHE *her dressing-gown.*) The sea is calm and the water's piling up as if it had been in the storm. Everything's open and new. (*Coffee cup.*) There's a stain in this cup. Take it into the kitchen and wash it.

ANN: It's nothing. I'll drink from it.

MARTHE: No. Wash it. Respect things. Use them properly.

ANN *goes.* MARTHE *wraps herself in her dressing-gown and cuts bread.* ANN *comes back with coffee, milk, the cup and water for the petunia.*

What will you do if your mother asks you to move to the hotel. It's lonely to be on your own. I'd hate it.

ANN: You weren't *that* horrible to her. The quarrel is between you.

MARTHE (*slightly amused*): She'll say I stole her daughter.

ANN: She knows if I stay it's because I want to.

MARTHE: Pour the milk in a jug. (*She pours.*) A jug to make the table beautiful.

ANN: You're making washing-up.

MARTHE: Good. I won't see many more

beautiful things. You'll be sad for a few days and then your life will go on again. It will be beautiful. You'll think of me with fondness. Put a chair in front of each place.

ANN: How d'you know it will be beautiful?

MARTHE (*working*): What's more useless than death? Life without death would be. How could you find anything beautiful if you looked at it forever? You'd grow tired of it. Why fall in love if it lasted forever? When you'd forgiven yourselves a thousand times you'd tire of forgiveness. You'd grow tired of changing the people you loved. If you ate for eternity why bother to taste what you're eating? You can taste the next meal. When you've cried for one mistake you wouldn't cry for the next. You'd have eternity to put it right. Soon your eyes would be full of sleep. You'd go deaf. You wouldn't listen to voices because they would give you the trouble of answering. Why listen to them? It would be useless to know which was a bird or a waterfall. In eternity there would be no future. You'd sit on the ground and turn to stone. Dust would pile up and bury you. If we didn't die we'd live like the dead. Without death there's no life. No beauty, love or happiness. You can't laugh for more than a few hours or weep more than a few days. No one could bear more than one life. Only hell could be eternal. Sometimes life is cruel and death is sudden – that's the price we pay for not being stones. Don't let the lightning strike you or madmen burn your house. Don't give yourself to your enemies or neglect anyone in need. Fight. But in the end death is a friend who brings a gift: life. Not for you but the others. I die so that you might live. Did you call David? Breakfast's ready.

ANN: I didn't dry the cup.

MARTHE: Let me.

ANN *goes and* MARTHE *dries the cup. She smooths a corner of the table with her hand, goes to the chair, pulls the wrap round her legs and sleeps. The* GERMAN *comes up from the street. He carries a bunch of flowers wrapped in florist's cellophane and tied with yellow ribbon.*

GERMAN: Speak German? . . . Dear Lady. (*He coughs.*) The taxi is taking us to the airport. If we miss the plane . . . It's part of a package. (*He touches* MARTHE's *wrist. No response. He wanders round the terrace. Calls louder to the house.*) Hello. (*To* MARTHE:) Pst! (*To himself:*) Tch tch. If I wake the lady will she be angry?

VOICE (*off, calls*): Vati!

GERMAN (*calls*): Soon! There's a good girl, Haidi! (*He smacks his hands together as if reprimanding a child and calls:*) Shush! (*He turns to* MARTHE:) The children are cross. I insisted to come up. Now the taxi's ticking over. The driver will charge extra. Sigi will sulk on the plane. (*Slightly tearfully.*) Only to press her hand . . .

He goes to the table, spreads jam on bread and eats it. Off, a car horn. He puts the flowers down and goes. DAVID *comes in. He wears a dressing-gown. He sits at the table.* ANN *comes in.*

ANN: I thought I heard a call.

DAVID (*grunt*): Who?

ANN (*to* MARTHE): Marthe.

DAVID: Let her sleep.

ANN: She wanted to eat with us.

ANN *sits.* DAVID *pours coffee.*

DAVID: She ate some bread. Not taken her tablet.

ANN: She wouldn't tell me what they rowed about.

DAVID (*looks at his watch*): Your mother will.

ANN: Are you late?

DAVID: No.

ANN (*takes coffee*): Thank you.

DAVID: Don't go to the hotel.

ANN: I must see how my –

DAVID: To stay.

ANN: Oh, no, how could I?

DAVID (*her hand is on the table. He rests his head on it*): I don't want to come between you and her. She'll have you all the time when you're gone. (*He lifts his head.*)

ANN: She's not an ogress. She's kind if you let her.

DAVID: All things under the sun throw a shadow. Your mother throws hers towards the light.

ANN: Flowers (*She picks up the flowers.*) A delivery man. That's who I heard.

DAVID: Are they for you?

ANN: The envelope's written in German. (*She gives it to* DAVID.)

DAVID (*reads. Looks up*): For you. 'An das schöne Fräulein in weiss.' To the beautiful girl in white.

ANN: How amazing.

DAVID: You wear white.

ANN: Sometimes.

DAVID: Expensive.

ANN *opens the envelope, takes out a letter and gives it to* DAVID.

DAVID (*reads*): Merciful lady – (*He looks up.*) A common form of address in the German tongue. (*He reads.*) I could not end our holiday in your beautiful homeland without writing this letter. Not till after dinner on that memorable day did I realise I had again met the beautiful girl in white we gazed on so long ago. Believe an old but still active man when he speaks from the heart of the great debt he owes you. Merciful lady I understand why you did not speak to me on the boat. Happily you now understand the cause of my disrespect. When I deliver these flowers I shall press your hand in silence and let them speak for me. You will be gratified to learn that Sigi and Haidi are safe. Their boat ran out of petrol. Friendly fishermen took them in tow. Alas there will be no time to present them to you. I have told them of our memorable meeting and will do so again many times in the years ahead. To the beautiful girl in white on the balcony of long ago with the humble respects of her dutiful Heinrich Hemmel. P.S. I am innocent. (*He stops reading.*) With an address.

ANN: They're for my mother. Some old flame. The balcony of long ago. What can it mean?

DAVID: The German we took in the boat. Put them in water.

ANN *goes out.* DAVID *takes a tablet and glass of water to* MARTHE. *He puts the*

*tablet and glass on the floor. He feels her
pulse. He kneels in front of her.* XENIA
comes in. She carries a light jacket.

XENIA: David.

DAVID *presses* MARTHE*'s hands
against his face, kisses them and covers his
hands with them.*

DAVID: She's warm. Her hands are still
warm.

ANN *comes back with a large blue vase.*
DAVID *begins to cry.*

Still warm. Give me something to cover
her hands. Keep her warmth in. Don't let
it go! Let me feel her warmth!

XENIA (*to* ANN): Is she – ?

DAVID: Help me! Anything! Anything!
Her warmth will go!

ANN *takes* XENIA*'s jacket and gives it to*
DAVID. *He covers* MARTHE*'s hands
with it and presses his head against it.*

XENIA: I'm sorry. – We had a quarrel.
After a dreadful day on the island.

ANN: Go back to the hotel.

XENIA: No no I must stay. There are things
to do. You'll need me.

ANN: Wait there. I'll come to you. Your
flowers. (*She gives them to* XENIA.)

XENIA: Don't push me like that!

ANN: Please mother!

XENIA: As you wish. I'll send for my
things. I won't put you to that trouble.
You'll have enough to do.

ANN: Go go. I'll come soon. I won't be
long.

XENIA: Stay here. I don't need you. I
telephoned Daddy last night to say I'd
come home today. Of course I'll stay for
the funeral. What are these ugly flowers?
(*She gives the flowers back to* ANN.) I'm
sorry she's dead. I came to tell her I
wasn't angry. My presence filled her with
a great rage. It was bad for someone in
her condition. If I'd known I'd never have
come here.

XENIA *goes.*

DAVID (*presses* MARTHE*'s hands to his
head. Cries*): Bless me. Bless me. Still
warm . . .

DAVID *presses* MARTHE*'s hands to his
head and face, and covers his eyes with
them.*
ANN *watches him for a moment and then
goes.*
DAVID *kneels before* MARTHE *and
cries in her lap.*

Seven

The house. Day.
MARTHE*'s chair has been taken away.*
ANN *sits at the table and mechanically
drinks coffee.*
DAVID *comes in.*

ANN: Shouldn't you lie down?

DAVID: No.

ANN: I'll come and hold you.

DAVID: I'm all right.

He sits at the table. ANN *pours coffee. He
takes it but doesn't drink.*

I've seen so many deaths. I cried for them
all this morning.

ANN: I shall go back to England soon. I
must find a new job.

DAVID: Perhaps we deceived ourselves.
There may be no child.

ANN: I don't know yet.

DAVID: If there is will you keep it?

ANN: Yes.

DAVID: Alone?

ANN: If I have to.

DAVID: You must tell it I'm its father.

ANN: If it grew up I'd bring it to you.
Mother must go to the funeral.

DAVID (*drinks coffee*): If you weren't here
I'd say no. It's as you please.

ANN: Did she say where her ashes were to
be thrown?

DAVID: In the garden.

ACH ENTERTAINM

the BEATLES

SHOW

RIALTO BALLROOM STANHO LIVERPO

THU 6T

7.3

ARRING THE ROCK C

THE BEATLE

TO THE FIRST MERSEYSIDE
PEARANCE FOLLOWING HIS
SON AT BUTLINS SKEGNESS

RORY

AND THE BIG

The Merse

BUFFET

THE
BEATLES

THE
BEATLES

A Photographic History of the Fab Four

Photographs by

Daily Mail

Bath · New York · Cologne · Melbourne · Delhi
Hong Kong · Shenzhen · Singapore · Amsterdam

This edition published by Parragon Books Ltd 2014

Parragon
Chartist House
15–17 Trim Street
Bath BA1 1HA, UK
www.parragon.com

Text © Parragon Books Ltd 2010–2014
Photographs © Associated Newspapers Archive and Hulton Archive/Getty Images (see page 256)

Produced by Atlantic Publishing
Design by John Dunne

Cover design by five-twentyfive.com

ISBN 978-1-4723-3209-7

Printed in China

Contents

Introduction

Four lads who shook the world

Revisiting past glories and pleasures can often be an unrewarding experience. The glitter of any golden age tarnishes all too easily; the treasures of youth can appear dated and embarrassing just a few short years later. Those who were swept along with the tide of Osmondmania or Rollermania may have fond memories of the time, but it's doubtful whether the tartan cut-offs or "Puppy Love" get much of an airing today.

The Beatles had more than their share of hype and hysteria; all the trappings and excesses of pop superstardom were there. They didn't have to play a note to send audiences into raptures and once the audience was in raptures, the notes were hardly worth playing. The deafening screams swamped the puny Vox amplifiers in those early days and the four of them sometimes gave in and stopped performing. The fans appeared not to realize—or to care.

But after Beatle jackets and haircuts were outgrown, after the flimflam and froth were stripped away, there remained the unique melding of four individual talents. They produced a canon of work with a timeless quality, music for all succeeding generations to discover and enthuse over. It is said that Brian Wilson, the creative genius behind the Beach Boys, abandoned the project he was working on after hearing *Sgt. Pepper* for the first time. He didn't see the point of going on now that the definitive album had been made.

The Beatles not only dominated the musical landscape during their years together, but influenced it immeasurably after they went their separate ways. At the site of the original Cavern Club in Mathew Street there is a legend which puts it succinctly: "Four lads who shook the world." A Photographic History of *The Beatles* recaptures that seismic phenomenon.

CHAPTER ONE

The Early Years
Ticket To Ride

Everyone knows that The Beatles came from Liverpool, but their distinctive sound and their talent for reaching an audience came not from the bars and clubs of their home town, but from their exhaustive stints far away in Hamburg. Until they went to Germany, the band was a constantly changing collection of part-time musicians, with a hard core of three members: John Lennon and Paul McCartney, both on rhythm guitar, and George Harrison on lead. They played anywhere they could—private parties, youth clubs, working men's clubs—not only changing the lineup regularly, but also experimenting with different names for the group.

Until 1960 the band had no permanent drummer or a bass guitarist, so when John's art-college friend Stu Sutcliffe won £60 in an art contest he was promptly persuaded to invest in a bass guitar even though he couldn't play. The band had earlier met local club-owner Allan Williams, who began to book them into gigs round Liverpool and even got them an audition which led to a short tour round Scotland, backing singer Johnny Gentle. In the middle of 1960, Williams was looking for another group to send to Hamburg and the only one available to go was… The

Beatles. He offered them the booking, on condition they found themselves a competent drummer. One of their regular venues was the Casbah Club and Pete Best, son of the owner, had his own drum kit. He was quickly recruited into The Beatles, and off they went to Germany.

In Hamburg the five Beatles John, Paul, George, Stu, and Pete—had to play ridiculously long hours every night in the same venue in front of demanding customers. They not only became a much more tightly knit group, they also had to develop a dynamic stage presence and a louder, more raunchy playing style to satisfy the often drunken audience. Another major influence on their style was photographer Astrid Kirchherr, who took atmospheric pictures of them around the city and cut Stu's hair into the famous mop-top later adopted by John, Paul, and George.

In addition, the band expanded their repertoire and came to know the songs so well that they were

Opposite: The sweet smile of success. At the end of 1962, Brian Epstein had been buying up copies of "Love Me Do" by the bucketload to ensure chart success; within a few short months, advance copies of Beatles records were selling in their hundreds of thousands.

able to develop and perfect the sound that later took the world by storm. The line-up was also soon on its way to the final four: Stu left the group to live with Astrid, leaving Paul to take over bass guitar, and they became friendly with Ringo Starr, who was in Hamburg with Rory Storm and the Hurricanes. After The Beatles returned to Liverpool at the end of 1960, they were booked to appear at Litherland Town Hall. Their new sound and extrovert stage show exploded onto a stunned British audience, and things were never the same again.

It was not long before word of this dynamic new group spread round Liverpool and came to the ears of Brian Epstein, a local businessman and record-store owner. He came to see them at the Cavern Club one lunchtime and promptly decided he wanted to manage them—even though he had never managed a band before. He immediately took the boys in hand, making sure they turned up to bookings on time, tidying up their stage show, and getting rid of their "greasy rocker" image by banning their leather gear and putting them all into suits. He also started looking for a recording contract and finally got the group an audition at Decca—who turned them down. Brian was incensed, but he didn't give up and in May 1962 George Martin of Parlophone finally agreed to take them on.

One problem still remained—Martin was not keen on Pete Best's drumming style. This could perhaps have been resolved, but George, Paul, and John took it as an opportunity to get rid of Pete, who they felt didn't fit in, and invite Ringo to join them instead. Pete had been with them for nearly two years but none of them was prepared to tell him to his face, so they left the task to Brian. It was all handled very badly.

Ringo joined The Beatles in mid-August, so he had just over two weeks of playing with them before they recorded their first single, "Love Me Do"/"PS I Love You." It was released in October and managed to reach No. 17 in the charts—if rumors are to be believed, mainly because Brian Epstein bought up 10,000 copies.

Although The Beatles now had one record out and were due to appear on their first London TV program, they were still almost completely unknown outside Merseyside—but not for long. Throughout 1963 they worked a punishing schedule, which included four national British concert tours, two Scottish tours, one short Swedish tour, and numerous one-night shows. They made two LPs, three EPs, and four singles, a multitude of TV and radio recordings, and attended many photographic sessions and Press interviews. No reasonable request for their time was refused by Brian Epstein. Their second single was released early in the year and, after a rapid climb, hit the number-one spot toward the end of February. At the time The Beatles were on a tour supporting Helen Shapiro, but gradually they became the major attraction. For the following tour they were supposed to be supporting two American stars, Tommy Roe and Chris Montez, but soon took over as top of the bill.

In August, The Beatles gave their last-ever show at the Cavern; it could no longer contain the vast crowds of Beatle fans and anyway they had outgrown their local following. The BBC were not slow to pick up on the group's growing popularity: after many radio show appearances, the boys were offered their own radio series, *Pop Go The Beatles*, which ran over four weekly programs. The Beatles also appeared on BBC television so many times that cynics began to dub it the "Beatles Broadcasting Corporation." They already had their own monthly magazine, *The Beatles Book*, and an official fan club, which had grown from a few thousand to 80,000 paid-up members by the end of 1963.

Even early in the year, Beatle-inspired mania had begun to break out locally around Britain, although it was only in October that the national newspapers finally began to pick up on the story. A live appearance by The Beatles on the network TV show, *Val Parnell's Sunday Night at the London Palladium*, which led to crowds of hysterical fans gathering outside the normally staid theater in the center of London, finally caught their attention. The next day the papers were full of stories about fans rioting and breaking through a police cordon when the boys tried to leave the theater. A couple of weeks later The Beatles returned to Heathrow from a short tour of Sweden and were stunned by the thousands of fans who had gathered in the rain to welcome them back, along with a full complement of reporters and photographers.

Since the national fame of The Beatles had arrived so suddenly, they soon found themselves having to fulfill bookings made months previously for fees that were ludicrously low in comparison to what they could now command. Brian Epstein did occasionally try to buy them out of some of these dates if he thought that the proposed venue would no longer be safe, but otherwise he never went back on a signed contract. A much more serious problem was the increasingly manic behavior of the fans, which had now become dangerous both to themselves and the group. Girls cried, screamed, tried to throw themselves at their favorite Beatle or grab pieces of clothing or snippets of hair, or simply fainted. Even in the small town of Carlisle, 600 fans lined up for up to 36 hours in freezing weather for the box office to open. When it did, the surge forward resulted in nine people being taken to hospital. At larger venues the casualties sometimes ran into hundreds. It was a major logistical exercise to get the band to and from the venue in safety, and once inside they had to stay cooped up in their dressing-rooms, prisoners of their own fame. When thay actually made it onto the stage, they had to dodge around to avoid being hit by the gifts and packets of jelly babies thrown by fans.

For The Beatles themselves the growing Beatlemania was at first flattering, but quickly went beyond a joke and began to be a cause of some resentment. Concert tours were already a mind-numbing routine of arriving in a town, being smuggled into the venue, performing a show, being hustled out into a van for a high-speed getaway to a nearby hotel, and then holing up overnight until it

was time to go through it all again the next day. They had to wear elaborate disguises to go out in public, their homes and those of their families were under constant siege from fans, articles were stolen from their dressing-rooms, and the piercing screams throughout concerts meant that no one—not even The Beatles themselves—could hear the music.

But they had already changed the British music scene for ever. Before this, popular musical trends had invariably started in America and major stars were American, while London had a stranglehold on the British scene. Now Liverpool suddenly became fashionable and Merseyside took over the pop charts. Gerry and the Pacemakers, Cilla Black, the Searchers, Billy J. Kramer and the Dakotas all owed their success to The Beatles—and most of them were also managed by Brian Epstein.

Below: George dances the night away at a party given by millionaire John Bloom.

"I haven't seen anything like this..."

Paul and John's prodigious songwriting talent comes to the fore in 1963. They begin the year by stubbornly refusing George Martin's suggestion to record "How Do You Do It?" as a follow-up to "Love Me Do," insisting on writing their own material. (Gerry and the Pacemakers were subsequently offered the song and took it to No. 1 in the charts.)

Below: After their triumphant appearance on *Sunday Night at the London Palladium*, the boys try to wrong-foot fans by leaving via the front exit, rather than the stage door. Ringo, John, Paul, and road manager Neil Aspinall show concern as they emerge to find no waiting vehicle.

Opposite above: The getaway car has been parked some way up Argyll Street, where police hoped it would look less conspicuous. By the time Paul and Ringo reach it, the fans are in hot pursuit. "I haven't seen anything like this since Johnny Ray appeared in 1955," said George Cooper, the theater's stage doorman.

Opposite below: The Beatles in an off-duty moment at a TV studio in Birmingham. The hectic touring commitments continue, but Epstein recognizes the impact of television exposure. Record sales quadruple on the day following the Palladium appearance, and Epstein is already targeting the top-rated *Ed Sullivan Show* as a bridgehead for The Beatles' assault on America.

"Rattle your jewelry"

Left and below: Thousands of fans gather at London Airport as the Beatles return from a five-day trip to Sweden. They create a bigger security headache than Prime Minister Sir Alec Douglas-Home, who happens to be passing through the airport at the same time. By pure chance, one witness to the chaotic scenes is the very person Epstein wants to do business with—Ed Sullivan himself.

Opposite: Rehearsing on November 4 for the Royal Variety Performance at the Prince of Wales Theatre. The nineteen-act bill includes Max Bygraves, Harry Secombe, Tommy Steele, Marlene Dietrich, and Pinky and Perky. The Beatles are seventh on stage but, predictably, steal the show with a set comprising "From Me To You," "She Loves You," "Till There Was You," and "Twist and Shout." However, the evening is probably best remembered for the celebrated "ad lib" with which John introduces the final number: "Will those in the cheaper seats clap your hands; the rest of you can just rattle your jewelry."

Mop-tops...

Bottom: Close-up mop-top. Beatles wigs are just one example of the vast merchandising industry which accompanies Beatlemania. Epstein fails to realize the full potential of this market. He enters into an agreement in which 90 percent of merchandising profits go to a company set up to handle all such matters. One of the earliest deals was with a clothing company which paid $100,000 for the right to produce Beatle T-shirts. Epstein thought this sum ludicrous, until he discovered that the company recouped this outlay in just three days. It would be 1967 before this disastrous arrangement was ended, by which time it was estimated that The Beatles had lost $100 million.

Top right and top left: Ringo dances with music publisher's wife Mrs Lou Levy at a Mayfair party given by millionaire John Bloom. 68-year-old porter Arthur Dyer proves to be slightly out of touch with popular culture by refusing to let The Beatles in at first, believing them to be gatecrashers instead of VIP guests.

Opposite: There is no better endorsement for a garment than to have a Beatle wear it. Here, as the boys arrive for a concert in Huddersfield, Ringo sports a corduroy coat. The ailing corduroy industry is said to have The Beatles to thank for a huge growth in sales during this period.

Right: The Beatles are very thinly disguised as policemen in order to get past the huge crowds gathering for a concert outside the Birmingham Hippodrome.

A quiet night out

Right and far right: Paul's hopes for a quiet evening out with Jane Asher are dashed as he becomes the center of attention at a West End theater.

Below: George sends another autograph-hunter away happy. The first Harrison song to feature on a Beatles record is "Don't Bother Me" on the LP *With The Beatles.*

Flying high in the charts

Swapping a drumstick for a joystick. Ringo tries his hand at the controls of the Viking aircraft taking some of the biggest names in pop from Liverpool to London. Brian Epstein had chartered the plane at a cost of £400 to give Ringo and other members of his Mersey Sound stable a break from *The Beatles' Christmas Show*, at the Astoria, Finsbury Park.

The Beatles had cause to be pleased with themselves in December '63. Advance sales of their new single, "I Want To Hold Your Hand," hit the one million mark, while orders for the new LP *With The Beatles* stand at 250,000—a record for an album.

CHAPTER TWO

1964

A Hard Day's Night

If 1963 was the year that Beatlemania hit Britain, 1964 was the year when The Beatles conquered the rest of the world. Their first stop was Paris, but the shows here were not a success. The Beatles themselves were not satisfied with how things were organized, nor with their playing at the first concert, and one of the amplifiers cut out so many times that sabotage was suspected. The audience at the second concert was mainly Parisiennes in evening dress, rather than young rock fans, so the band received a cool reception. This was the concert the French Press attended, so reviews were similarly cool. These problems did not affect them long, however, as news suddenly came by telegram that "I Want To Hold Your Hand" had shot from No. 43 to No. 1 in the music charts in America.

Soon all the group's records were climbing up the American charts—just days before they were due to visit New York to appear on The Ed Sullivan Show and to give concerts at the Washington Coliseum and Carnegie Hall. Their reception at John F. Kennedy Airport was wildly enthusiastic, as America succumbed to The Beatles in a typically whole-hearted fashion. The viewing figures for The Ed Sullivan Show smashed the existing world record for the largest-ever audience for an entertainment show, and during The Beatles' ten-minute spot there were no hub

caps reported stolen in New York—which was also a first!

As well as visiting New York and Washington The Beatles spent a few days in Miami, where they not only appeared live on The Ed Sullivan Show again and taped a third performance to be shown later, but also managed a few days of rest and relaxation. Wherever the boys went the now-familiar scenes of pandemonium unfolded yet again as American fans went crazy.

After their brief visit to America, the group returned home to begin their first movie, A Hard Day's Night, at Twickenham. The storyline was based on incidents from their own lives, with all four Beatles playing their parts with great confidence. Meanwhile, Beatlemania was taking hold across the rest of the world. By the beginning of April, Beatles singles occupied the top five positions in the American Billboard chart and the top six positions in the singles charts in Sydney.

After four weeks off in May, the longest rest The Beatles had managed for some considerable time, they were ready to begin their first world tour, starting in Denmark. The day before their departure Ringo collapsed during a photo-shoot and was rushed to hospital suffering from tonsillitis and pharyngitis. Although George felt that they couldn't go without Ringo and wanted to cancel the tour, Brian Epstein and George Martin persuaded him that this was impossible. Instead, Jimmy Nicol, a very experienced but relatively unknown session drummer, became the temporary replacement for Ringo. Just hours after Ringo's collapse, Nicol went to EMI's Abbey Road studios to rehearse six numbers with the world's greatest supergroup and the following day he was on his way to Denmark.

Beatlemania now followed the band wherever they appeared, not just at the concert venues in Denmark, The Netherlands, Hong Kong, Australia, and New Zealand but also wherever the plane touched down for refueling. Day or night, in even the remotest of places, crowds of screaming fans appeared out of nowhere to try and catch a glimpse of their idols. Ringo rejoined The Beatles in Australia, just in time for their first concert in Melbourne. Their reception across the country was even more manic than it had been in America: in Melbourne, an estimated 250,000 people gathered outside their hotel and in Adelaide the crowd was over 300,000—many more than had ever turned out to see them in either Britain or even in America.

After a few bookings in Britain and another short tour to Sweden, The Beatles then set off on their first full American tour. It consisted of 32 shows in 24 cities within 34 days—which would perhaps have been reasonable in Britain, but was far too much in a land the size of America. John, Paul, George, and Ringo spent almost the entire time travelling and, except for journeying to and from concert venues and airports, they were unable to leave their hotels. They saw very little of any of the places they visited, only the crowds of rampaging fans everywhere they went.

Kansas City was not originally included in the tour, but Charles O. Finlay, the millionaire president of the Kansas City Athletics baseball team, was determined to get The Beatles for his city and offered the unprecedented sum of $150,000 for them to appear for one night at Kansas City Stadium. After their visit, the 16 sheets and eight pillowcases from their hotel beds were sold to two Chicago businessmen for $750. The linen was left unlaundered, cut into three-inch squares, mounted on a card with a legal affidavit and sold at $10 a time. The towels used by The Beatles to mop their faces after the concert were also cut up and sold.

When The Beatles returned to Britain from America, to the usual hysterical scenes at London Airport, the Prime Minister, Sir Alec Douglas-Home, called them "our best exports" and "a useful contribution to the balance of payments."

Left: Seeing double—The Beatles and their waxwork equivalents at Madame Tussaud's.

Previous spread: Paul, George, Ringo, and John enjoy some winter sunshine in Miami at the end of their first trip to the USA.

Opposite: George gets a hair cut in preparation to take the US by storm.

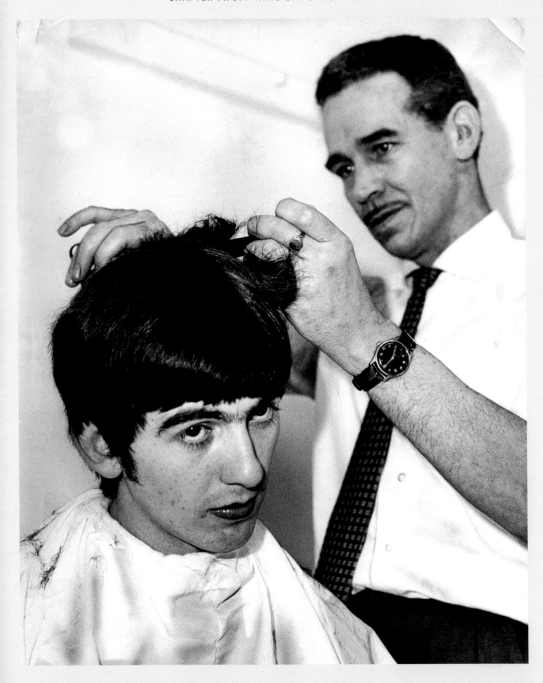

She loves you...

Below: George takes advantage of a brief respite in the relentless schedule to return home to Liverpool.

Harold and Louise Harrison help him pack for the America trip. Some of George's gear goes into his "BEA-TLES" travel bag, the airline company's latest merchandising gimmick. In return for displaying the bags prominently, the boys were given free flights between London and Paris.

Mum and number one fan Louise, who encouraged his early efforts with the guitar and attended a lot of the early gigs.

Opposite: John and George on their way to France, where lukewarm audiences get the year off to an inauspicious start. Throughout their 18-day residency at the Olympia Theater, Paris, Sylvie Vartan and American singer Trini Lopez go down better than The Beatles with the French audiences. However, the boys are buoyed by the news that they have become the first British group to top the US charts with "I Want to Hold Your Hand."

Right: The Lennons at London Airport, preparing to fly out to New York. The fact that one of the Beatles was married with a child had only recently been uncovered by prying reporters.

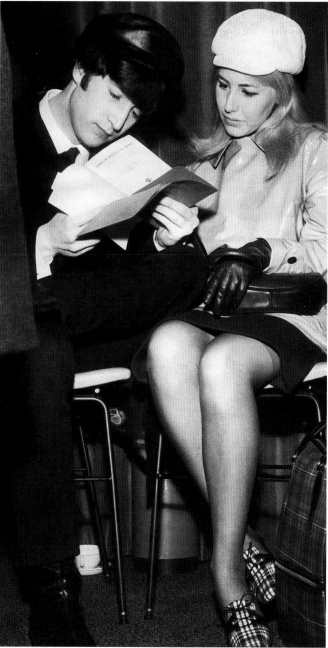

The Beatles Are Coming!

"The Beatles Are Coming!" That was the message on hoardings and on the airwaves right across the USA.

Apart from the two *Ed Sullivan Show* appearances, The Beatles give just three performances during their 15-day America trip: one concert at Washington Coliseum, and two shows at Carnegie Hall.

The Washington venue had the boys on a revolving stage. This had unfortunate consequences, for it not only afforded the whole audience a better view, but it also made the group a target to a lot more people. It had been reported that George had a particular weakness for jelly babies; this fondness proved painful in Washington, for the stage was peppered from all angles with these mini-missiles.

The Beatles were doing their best to belt out their material, but their Vox amplifiers were nowhere near up to the task in a venue full of screaming teenagers.

**Washington:
Look this way boys...**

More photo calls on their flying visit.

The two Carnegie Hall concerts are hugely successful and massively over-subscribed, and as a result there was a last-minute attempt to organize a show at Madison Square Garden—at double the Carnegie Hall fee—but this proved impossible.

Seeing the sights

Reviews of *The Ed Sullivan Show* are mixed,
including this from the *New York Journal-American*:
"Sartorially they're silly, tonsorially they're wildly
sloppy, musically they're not quite hopeless." The
estimated 73 million audience begs to differ.

Epstein had targeted the top-rated show to
get exposure for the group, after "Love Me Do,"
"Please Please Me," and "She Loves You" had
all failed to make an impression. The *Sullivan
Show* wanted the Beatles as a novelty support
act; Epstein wanted a top-of-the-bill slot. The
deal ultimately thrashed out—headlining two
shows on consecutive weeks for a total fee of
just $7000. Epstein used the show as a huge
loss-leader in order to break into the US market.

Miami

A far cry from ferrying across the Mersey. The boys go cruising off the Miami coast aboard the luxury yacht *Southern Trail*. Their second appearance on *The Ed Sullivan Show*, on February 16, is another triumph, with the audience again hitting the 70 million mark.

Miami beach boys

The fact that the schedule during the visit is, by Beatles' standards, not very onerous leaves the boys plenty of time to hit Miami beach before their second appearance on the *Sullivan Show*.

The dignified distance that most of the onlookers keep belies the frenzy that sweeps across America during this first visit. Anything Beatle-related is suddenly in demand and over half a ton of Beatle wigs and 24,000 rolls of Beatle wallpaper are quickly flown to America.

In the US, "I Want To Hold Your Hand" had become the fastest-selling single to date when it sold 250,000 copies within the first three days of its release. In March, "Can't Buy Me Love" was released with advance orders of over two million in the US alone.

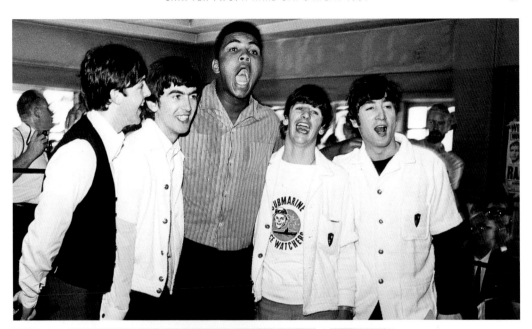

The Greatest

The Beatles come up against Cassius Clay, who is in Miami for his February 25 world title showdown with Sonny Liston. Clay declares that he's still the greatest, but The Beatles are the prettiest. Both parties come to world prominence in 1964 and go on to dominate their respective fields for the rest of the decade.

Above: Waiting for "The Greatest," Cassius Clay.

The Beatles returned to England on February 22. A 36-minute documentary program on their US visit was shown on British television while they were away.

Left and opposite: Making a publicity appearance in the US under the watchful eye of Brian Epstein.

21 today!

George receives 52 sacks of mail containing 15,000 cards on his 21st birthday. Presents inevitably include endless packets of jelly babies, but one fan sends a full-sized door for George to put his 21st birthday key in.

Opposite, above and far right: Helping George to deal with the mountain of mail are Beatles' Fan Club secretaries Anne Collingham (left) and Bettina Rose.

Right: Around the time of George's 21st birthday, The Beatles taped an appearance for the variety show *Big Night Out*.

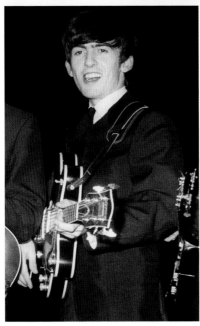

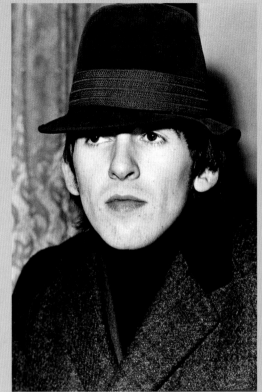

A visit to Oxford

Opposite below: With filming for *A Hard Day's Night* just under way, the boys are invited to dine at Brasenose College, Oxford. John recollects his Chaucer studies at school; George trades his smoked salmon for jelly sandwiches. (l to r: Paul, George, student Michael Lloyd, principal Sir Noel Hall, tutor Mr David Stockton, Ringo, John).

Opposite above right: Ringo with Sir Noel Hall.

Opposite above left: George goes incognito with his mop-top well covered.

Right: Ringo on set at 6.00 am at the Turk's Head, Twickenham. The pub is renamed the Liverpool Arms for the movie, with a street market to add dockland authenticity. The movie's working title is still *Beatlemania* and thousands of Liverpudlian fans protest that the movie should have been made in the group's home town.

Opposite above: Paul and George attend a Pickwick Club party for Sammy Davis Jnr.
Accompanying them are actresses Hayley Mills and Jane Asher, Paul's new girlfriend. Ringo's early-
morning set call (this page) prevents him from accompanying them.

Opposite below: Paul and Jane chatting to dancer Lionel Blair and comedian Dickie Henderson at
the Pickwick Club party.

A Hard Day's Night

Right: These four lucky girls not only appear in The Beatles' movie as fans, but also get the job of running their combs through the most famous hair in the world. No wonder it's smiles all round from (l to r) Pattie Boyd, Tina Williams, Pru Bury, and Susan Whiteman.

Below: Paul relaxes at the piano during a break from filming at Twickenham Studios.

"The Nation is Proud"

The Beatles win the Variety Club Show Business Personality of the Year award for 1963. The luncheon ceremony, held at the Dorchester Hotel, is hosted by Harold Wilson.

The Labour Party leader presented the awards on March 19: "I will refrain from making political capital out of The Beatles... we are all proud of the creation of a new musical idiom in the world of communications."

Wilson takes a sideswipe at Prime Minister Sir Alec Douglas-Home's recent comments regarding The Beatles as a valuable export commodity for Britain.

Ready, Steady, Go!

Left: March 20 is Beatles night on television. The group perform live on ATV's *Ready, Steady, Go!*, with the Variety Club awards ceremony broadcast later the same evening.

Above right: The boys put their feet up during a break in filming at the Scala Theatre, while John takes the opportunity to publicize his book. Also pictured is producer Walter Shenson, who had negotiated a three-movie deal with Brian Epstein the previous fall. Shenson, working on behalf of United Artists, was hoping to exploit a loophole in The Beatles' EMI recording contract, which did not cover movie soundtracks. This meant that even if the movie bombed, there would be lucrative album sales to make up for it.

Above left, opposite above and opposite right: The Duke of Edinburgh presents the Carl-Alan awards at the Empire Ballroom, Leicester Square. The Beatles win two awards: Best Group of 1963, and Best Vocal Record, for "She Loves You."

Opposite left: Paul celebrates their latest honor with a Havana cigar. There's little time for resting on laurels, however. The following day sees the release of "Can't Buy Me Love," which goes straight to No. 1 on both sides of the Atlantic. Hardly surprising, as advance orders had been a world-record three million.

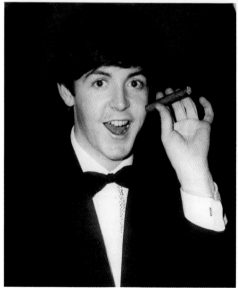

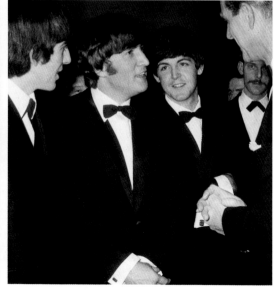

I'm happy just to dance with you...

Right: Member of Parliament Bessie Braddock gets a close-up view of what the Prime Minister calls "our best exports."

Opposite: Filming the nightclub scene at the exclusive Les Ambassadeurs Club, London, on April 17. The change in title from *Beatlemania* to *A Hard Day's Night* is announced in the media. Filming was hindered by a dispute over the unpaid extras used for the audience, which was only resolved when the 350 extras were given £3 15 shillings (£3.75) with lunch thrown in. Among their number was a callow youth who would go on to make his own mark in the world of popular music: one Phil Collins.

Below: Relaxing on a train.

Twist and shout

The Beatles assembled at Les Ambassadeurs Club in the afternoon to film the nightclub scene for *A Hard Day's Night*. Ringo is dancing (to "Twist and Shout") with Maggy London. Paul is in the background (*and opposite*) with Merrill Colebrook.

When asked to comment on the title change from *Beatlemania* to *A Hard Day's Night*, the producer said "It means something if you don't think about it too much."

Opposite below: John is guest of honor at a Foyle's literary luncheon on April 23, his book *In His Own Write* having been published a month earlier. John chats with Lionel Bart but disappoints the audience by declining to make a speech.

The Beatles and the Bard...

It's the Bard Beatle-style. The boys ham it up in a spoof version of *A Midsummer Night's Dream* for the TV show *Around The Beatles*. The show also featured them playing in their regular performance mode, and it was trailed that they would not be miming to their records. This was taken to equate to a live performance, but Epstein chose his words carefully. He was concerned about how The Beatles sounded on TV, so in this instance the group did indeed mime—but it was to a specially recorded set rather than the actual records.

Right: John at his Foyle's literary lunch.

Welcome to Edinburgh

When The Beatles arrive at Turnhouse airport, Edinburgh, on April 29 for the first of two consecutive nights in Scotland, they are presented with a lucky mascot by one of their young fans, Linda McLean.

Opposite: The concerts, in Edinburgh and in Glasgow, were promoted by Albert Bonici with Brian Epstein and were both hugely successful.

In person—The Beatles

Although a few lucky fans did meet The Beatles in person, the movie theater would not hold all those who had applied for tickets so there were hundreds of disappointed people outside just waiting for a glimpse of their idols. The concerts were so successful that The Beatles returned to Scotland in October, playing at Edinburgh, Dundee, and Glasgow during their UK tour.

Below and opposite below: Inside, the boys sign autographs and chat to a few of the lucky ones.

PS I Love You

Fame inevitably meant meeting fans and signing endless autographs, which
sometimes got The Beatles down, but in Edinburgh they seem to be enjoying all the
attention from some of their younger fans.

Just a few beers...

After a disastrous charity reception at the British Embassy in Washington, where The Beatles were pushed around by junior officials and ordered to sign autographs—and where one "distinguished" guest just walked up and snipped off a lock of Ringo's hair—the boys had refused to attend any more official functions. In Edinburgh, however, the Lord Provost sat down in the bar with them without any formality and a good time was had by all.

Opposite below: John takes a closer look at the heavy gold chain of office sported by the Lord Provost.

On stage at last

The Beatles played one concert in Edinburgh and two at
the Glasgow Odeon the following night.

"Which way to the stage?"

Opposite and below: "I tell you it's not that way!" The boys fool around for the cameras before they take to the stage.

While in Edinburgh, The Beatles also give an interview to BBC Scotland Radio reporter Bill Aitkenhead, which is broadcast that evening on the Scottish Home Service program *Scottish News*.

Right: Beatlemania Scottish style.

Below right: Autograph production line.

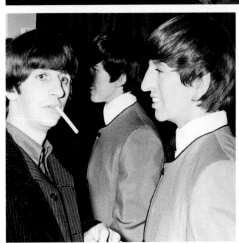

Face to face

Opposite: On April 29, The Beatles are on hand for the unveiling of their 1963-style effigies at Madame Tussaud's. The waxworks company's profits rocketed in the period following the inclusion of The Beatles.

Below: George and Pattie returning from vacation just prior to the world tour getting under way.

Right: Paul busy with autographs.

Around the world

The boys get together at the Prince of Wales Theatre on May 31 to announce their world tour. The first concert will be held in Copenhagen, Denmark, and they will then take in Australia and their first concert tour of America. They also plan five summer performances at British seaside resorts.

Cheers!

The Beatles drink to their forthcoming world tour at a Press conference held at the Prince of Wales Theatre in London.

Opposite bottom: Getting back in the groove; Paul preparing for two performances at the Prince of Wales Theatre.

Above and opposite above: The Beatles seemed to find themselves behind the bar for celebratory drinks on a regular basis—later in the year they toast the success of their UK tour, at the Odeon in Leeds.

Opposite below: Ringo puts on a brave face as he is admitted to University College Hospital, having collapsed at a photo-shoot earlier. After having his tonsil's removed, Ringo leaves hospital after a week, humming the latest Beatles' No. 1: "I Feel Fine" Just in case any ultra-determined fan has any designs on a rather exclusive, if ghoulish, piece of Beatles' memorabilia, he announces that the tonsils in question have been burned.

Jimmy in the nick of time...

Session drummer Jimmy Nicol gets rather more than 15 minutes of fame when he is called in as a last-minute replacement for Ringo, who is diagnosed as having tonsillitis and pharyngitis. A rehearsal at EMI Studios is hastily arranged, and Nicol gets the nod of approval.

Jimmy basks in the temporary limelight as he flies out to Denmark with John, George, and Paul. He had joined Georgie Fame's Blue Flames only the week before, but this part-tour would represent the pinnacle of his musical achievement. When Ringo rejoins the group in Australia, Nicol receives £500 and a gold watch before returning to relative obscurity.

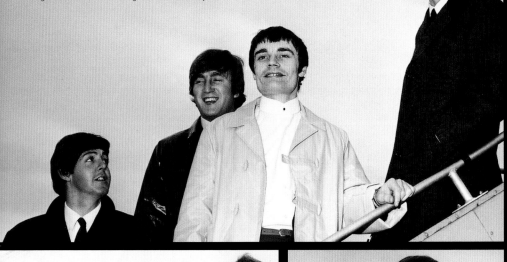

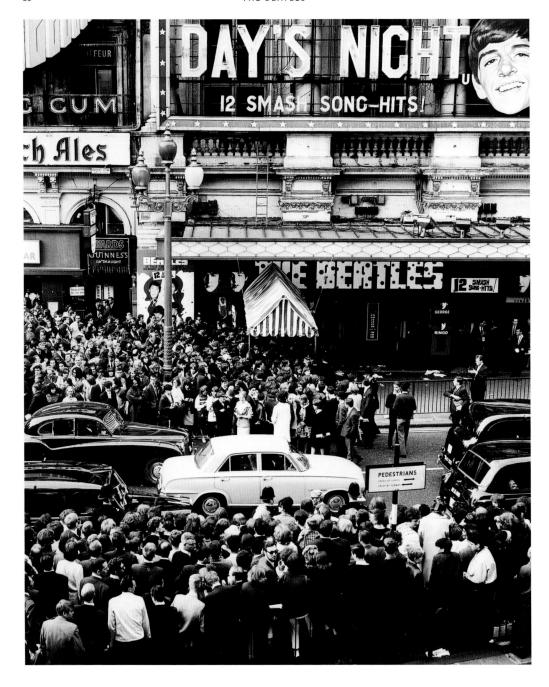

Liverpool lads

Opposite: Chaotic scenes outside the London Pavilion for the première of *A Hard Day's Night*.

Left: Princess Margaret meets the group at the première of *A Hard Day's Night* at the London Pavilion. The LP of the same name was released a couple of weeks later and went to the top of the charts. It was the first Beatles album to feature exclusively Lennon/McCartney compositions.

Above: Liverpool honors its four favorite sons. The Beatles are given a civic reception at the Town Hall, having attended the northern première of *A Hard Day's Night*.

Above and left: On stage in Dundee, during the Scottish leg of their UK tour.

Opposite: The Beatles are decked out for their Christmas show at the Hammersmith Odeon.

CHAPTER THREE

1965
Eight Days A Week

This year was really just more of the same for The Beatles. They released three singles, three EPs and two LPs and made a second movie, *Help!*, a comic-strip adventure about the attempts of an obscure Middle Eastern sect to recover a sacred sacrificial ring that a fan had sent to Ringo. This offered opportunities for location filming, so scenes in the Bahamas and Austria were written into the storyline. But the boys soon became bored during the long hours filming and turned to smoking pot to fill the time, so their concentration was not one hundred percent. Despite this, the movie was shot in under three months and was released within a further two months. It did good business and was well received by the critics.

Apart from filming and recording, the group's life was still dominated by touring, with a European tour to France, Italy, and Spain, another tour across America, and finally a short tour around Britain. All four Beatles had begun to feel that this relentless touring with its suffocating adulation was becoming almost impossible to bear. They were now subject to death threats and the unintentional terrorization by fans was getting even more out of hand. In Houston, Texas, at 2.00 in the morning, 5000 screaming teenagers broke through the airport barriers and a police cordon and were soon thronging round the plane, climbing on to the wings to peer through the windows and catch a glimpse of their idols. The Beatles were trapped and the pilot was unable to taxi the plane to safety as the fans were underneath it and around the wheels. The boys finally managed to escape through an emergency exit into a service truck and make their getaway.

During concerts John now quite regularly told the fans to "Shaddup!," and they discovered that even if one of them stopped playing for a few seconds no one noticed. Their music had suffered because of the impossibility of playing well under such conditions; they had once been proud of the fact that they were a tight group of accomplished musicians, but now hardly bothered to rehearse before a tour and often ended up playing abysmally at concerts. Who could blame them when everything was totally inaudible and no one seemed to be interested in listening anyway?

As they became increasingly angered by the mayhem around them, they began to turn their attention to pleasing themselves rather than their public. It was no longer possible to develop new songs on tour as they had in the old days, so they turned more to the recording studio and to working on a progressive complexity of sound. They told Brian Epstein that they wanted to give up touring, and vetoed his suggestions of another Royal Command Performance and another Christmas show. He managed to talk them into one more short tour of Britain that winter, which became the last that they ever did in the UK.

This was also the year in which The Beatles received their MBEs. The announcement was received with disbelief—not only by some of the battle-scarred previous recipients who returned their awards in disgust, but also by the group themselves. They assumed they had been honored for their services to the British export industry, rather than for playing rock music, but even so no pop

artiste had received such an award before. There was some talk initially about turning the honor down, as they all felt that it was too "Establishment," but in the end they accepted it.

On a personal note, by now each of them was settled with a partner. John and Cynthia had been married since 1962 and had a two-year-old son, while Ringo had married Maureen at the beginning of 1965 and their first son had just been born. Paul had been seeing actress Jane Asher since 1963 and George was living with model Pattie Boyd, whom he had met on the set of *A Hard Day's Night* in 1964. Although this didn't seem to affect the group's popularity, during the height of Beatlemania the wives and girlfriends were quite often subjected to abuse and attack from hysterical fans who were convinced that they alone were destined to be with their chosen Beatle.

But Beatlemania was finally beginning to show signs of running out of steam. In 1965, for the first time, some of the concert venues were not full to capacity and far fewer fans turned up at the airports to welcome the group or wave them a fond farewell. There were still plenty of fans, but perhaps they had begun to realize that it was a waste of money to pay for seats at a concert where their heroes could be as much as 500 yards away and at which they could not hear a note of the music. But The Beatles were still amazingly popular—as Newcastle University's Professor Strang said at the time, "You can walk down any street of the most primitive village in a country where no one speaks English and hear children chanting the words of the latest Beatles hit."

Previous spread: The Beatles are given a rapturous send-off at London Airport as they leave for the Bahamas, where shooting of their second movie is to begin.

Left: George inspects his MBE.

Opposite: Ringo and his new bride, 18-year-old former hairdresser Maureen Cox, pose for the cameras at Hove, Sussex, where they are honeymooning at a house owned by Beatles solicitor David Jacobs. The couple had married the previous day at Caxton Hall Register Office in London—at 8.00 am to avoid the fans.

Testing time

No more "watching the wheels" for John as he passes his driving test at the age of 24. He receives his congratulations in the EMI Studios parking lot, at the wheel of George Martin's car.

Eight arms to hold you...

Above: Actress Eleanor Bron is the envy of hordes of screaming teenage girls as she flies out to the Bahamas with The Beatles to costar in *Help!*. A leading light in the satirical comedy fringe, 26-year-old Miss Bron would not have experienced anything like the mass hysteria and adulation which accompanies the Fab Four.

Right and opposite: Cooling off in the Bahamas. The project went through several working titles, including *Eight Arms To Hold You*, before director Dick Lester came up with *Help!*.

Hot stuff

It's bikini weather in the Bahamas, and Paul (above) finds it hard to keep his eyes on the road.

Paul and George pictured at London Airport, a couple of weeks into the 11-week shooting schedule for *Help!*.

Paul and John take to the slopes

Above: Paul takes advantage of location filming in
Austria to try his hand at skiing. His instructor is Harriet
Davidson, niece of the Duke of Norfolk.

Right: John parts company with one of his skis during
a lesson at St. Moritz. In fact, John proved quite adept
on the slopes, staging the spill purely for the benefit of
impatient cameramen.

Opposite above: Radio Caroline DJ Simon Dee presents
the pirate station's First Birthday "Bell" Award to The
Beatles at Twickenham Film Studios.

Opposite below: The Mersey Sound hits Salisbury Plain.
Filming on a chilly May afternoon, with a backdrop of
Army personnel on maneuvers. Army sergeant Douglas
Gunn looks askance at two mop-tops.

Opposite: John and Eleanor Bron on location in Ailsa Avenue, Twickenham.

Above: Ringo does his best to keep warm between takes.

Birthday honors

Above: The calm before the storm. Paul gives the thumbs up as The Beatles become the first pop group to feature in the honors list. Many were astonished and angered by the news, however, regarding it as a debasement of the award. Behind the scenes, even the members of the group themselves had reservations about whether to accept.

Left: Off to check out the competition. Having completed filming on *Help!* a few days earlier, John flies out to the Cannes Film Festival, accompanied by Cynthia.

Opposite: Paul celebrates his 23rd birthday.

Help!

The Beatles in formal attire on the occasion of the royal charity première of *Help!* at the London Pavilion. "We'd be much happier in jeans and T-shirts," said George. Also pictured are Cynthia Lennon and Maureen Starr.

Opposite: John, Paul, and George acknowledge their fans as they return home from their second US tour. A few days earlier the idols had met their own idol—Elvis—at his Beverly Hills home in Perugia Way, but it was not to prove an enduring friendship.

Off to the Palace...

Opposite: Paul and Ringo head off to the Palace from Ringo's house in Montagu Square. Tradition favors top hat and tails on such occasions, but The Beatles opt for dark lounge suits to collect their MBEs.

Right: Leaving a besieged Buckingham Palace.

Below: The four show off their medals, following their investiture.

The Beatles, MBE

Even though news of the award had been in the public domain since June 12, the controversy surrounding the decision remained undiminished. The honor had been conferred at the personal recommendation of Prime Minister Harold Wilson, a self-confessed Beatles fan whose constituency was Huyton, Liverpool. But many agreed with critic Bernard Levin, who was incensed that such an honor should be awarded to four men whose music he regarded as "ephemeral rubbish." Some returned their own medals in protest.

Opposite below: Brian Epstein now proudly presents... The Beatles, MBE. Unlike The Beatles themselves, Epstein was unequivocal in his delight at the award. Investiture protocol meant that the four could have taken two guests each to the ceremony, but they decided to meet the Queen as a group, and only their manager was invited.

Day trippers

Opposite and left: The Beatles prepare for an ITV special celebrating the music of Lennon and McCartney. The show featured a string of guests performing Beatles songs, including Peter and Gordon ("A World Without Love," which went to the top of the charts); Marianne Faithfull ("Yesterday," which reached No. 36); Peter Sellers (reciting "A Hard Day's Night" in the style of Laurence Olivier's Richard III, which reached No. 14); and Lulu ("I Saw Him Standing There"). George and Ringo also got in on the act, joining Paul and John for a performance of their new single, "Day Tripper"/"We Can Work It Out."

Below: Paul, with Jane Asher. Speculation was rife that they were about to marry—or had done so already in secret.

CHAPTER FOUR

1966
Hello Goodbye

Although The Beatles had decided that they wanted to stop touring, as yet there had been no definite decision to quit so at first everyone expected 1966 to follow much the same format as the previous year. They did take a four-month break from live performances, using the time to work in the recording studio, but then a series of disasters turned the year into a nightmare for the band.

In March, the group had their official publicity photographs taken by Robert Whittaker. They were dressed normally in sweaters and dark jackets, but for some reason others were also taken with them all dressed up in butcher's white coats and posing with lumps of meat and dismembered dolls. One of these pictures was used in Britain to promote their new single, "Paperback Writer," without apparent comment, but the shot was also used for the cover of a new LP, *Yesterday And Today*, released by Capitol in America. When advance copies went out in mid-June and the photo started to appear on advertising billboards, there was an immediate outcry about its offensive nature. Capitol had to recall all copies and replace the picture with one showing the band standing round a suitcase, all of which cost them a fortune.

In the middle of this, The Beatles set out on a tour of West Germany, Japan, and the Philippines. The tour started well and they were warmly welcomed when they arrived in Hamburg after an absence of three years, but things began to go badly wrong on the way to Tokyo. First their flight was diverted because of a typhoon and had to touch down in Alaska for several hours. When The Beatles finally arrived in Japan they found themselves facing another storm: the local promoter had booked the Nippon Budokan, a magnificent hall that until then had been dedicated to traditional Japanese martial arts. Many Japanese considered it to be a sacred building and were horrified that it was to be used for Western pop music, with its screaming fans. Opposition to the concerts was bitter and there were angry demonstrations and marches. The police were out in force and each concert had 3000 officers strategically placed among the fans, ready to quell any pandemonium. As a result, 10,000 fans sat quietly to listen to the music—but by this time the band's level of musicianship had slipped so far that almost everything was mistimed and off-key.

The police also mounted an armed guard on the group's hotel, and they were forbidden to step outside. When they tried to slip out to view Tokyo, they were swiftly rounded up and returned to their rooms. John did escape briefly, but the security force then threatened to withdraw completely. If this was bad, things were to get much worse on their next stop in the Philippines.

Ferdinand and Imelda Marcos were at the height of their dictatorship when The Beatles arrived in Manila. The president, his wife and their three children were invited as guests of honor to the concerts and local papers reported that the band would be paying a courtesy call at the palace at 11.00 am. The boys were apparently not aware they were expected and didn't appear. They performed their two concerts, but the following morning the newspapers were full of stories about Imelda being "stood up," the British Embassy and The Beatles themselves received bomb and death threats, and the local promoter was so outraged that he refused to hand over the group's share of gate receipts. Brian Epstein quickly organized a televised apology explaining what had happened, but its transmission was mysteriously disrupted by a burst of static. The Philippines tax office refused to let anyone leave until they paid income tax on the concert revenue—which they still hadn't received—so Brian Epstein had to post a bond of £7000. They all then left for the airport, but their security forces had been withdrawn so they were kicked and jostled leaving the hotel and at the terminal. Minutes

after The Beatles had left Philippines soil, President Marcos issued a Press statement confirming that they had not intended to slight the First Lady.

A few weeks later there was yet more bad news. An American magazine had picked up an article in which John talked about religion, and in which he had said that The Beatles were more popular than Jesus. This had caused no comment in Britain at the time, but the American article paraphrased what he said out of context, reporting that he had said The Beatles were greater than Jesus. Within days the Bible Belt was in an uproar, with Beatles merchandise being ceremoniously burned and their music banned on local radio. This was just days before the start of their tour of America, and things became so fraught that it was nearly canceled.

In the event it did go ahead, starting with a Press conference at which John explained what he had said and apologized. Even so, the band received death threats and when a fire cracker exploded on stage at Memphis each of them was convinced that one of them had been shot. The final show was at Candlestick Park in San Francisco, where The Beatles played until exactly 10.00 pm and then left the stage. The touring was finally over.

Left: A kiss for Pattie from George on their wedding day.

Previous spread: The happy couple leaving the register office in Epsom.

A kiss for the bride

Below left: George, 22, marries 21-year-old Pattie Boyd at Epsom Register Office. It was Pattie's resemblance to Brigitte Bardot that first caught George's eye on the set of *A Hard Day's Night*, in which Pattie had a minor part. He had to be persistent, though—she was already engaged to somebody else at the time.

Pattie's red fox fur coat, by Mary Quant, is a wedding present from George; her gift to him is a set of George III wine goblets.

Below right: A kiss for the bride from the Beatles' one remaining bachelor. John and Ringo are still vacationing in the West Indies and send a telegram of congratulations. Not that they were missed by Registrar Leonard Clarke—he admits he is not a fan and can't tell one Beatle from another.

Above left and right: Any image change in a Beatle is newsworthy, but Ringo, complete with new beard, has no trend-setting thoughts. "I hate shaving, and while we're on holiday there's no need to," he says, as he and Maureen fly out to Trinidad. John and Cynthia join them in a mid-January break.

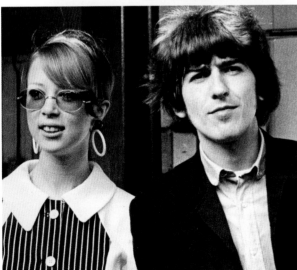

The perfect cook

George has married the perfect cook. That's his mother's opinion anyway. When asked about her cooking Pattie said, "I do enjoy cooking and am wondering what to prepare for George's Sunday meal." The happy bride revealed that she will continue modeling, but will not be doing as much as she has been.

Opposite below: The newlyweds, with Brian Epstein behind. He shares the best man duties with Paul.

Left and above: Two weeks after their wedding, George and Pattie leave for Barbados. "More of a holiday than a honeymoon," says George.

What's it all about...

Paul and Jane Asher arriving at a private preview of her new movie, *Alfie*. With them is Jane's brother Peter—of Peter and Gordon fame.

Opposite above: Not quite the fervor of a Beatles gig at the Italian Institue, Belgravia, as composer Luciano Berio introduces his latest work, *Un Omaggio a Dante* (A Homage To Dante.) But the audience does include a famous fellow musician sitting attentively in the front row. The reason? Signor Berio specializes in electronic music, and Paul has indicated that the Beatles are experimenting with different sounds on their new album, *Revolver*.

Opposite below: Paul and Jane Asher arriving at the Plaza Cinema, Haymarket, London, for the première of *Alfie*.

Last British Concert

The Beatles give what is to be their last British concert, at Empire Pool, Wembley, on May 1. A British tour had been penciled in for the end of the year, but this was eventually shelved, leaving the NME Poll Winners concert as the group's swan song for their home fans. It was a 15-minute, five-song set: "I Feel Fine," "Nowhere Man," "Day Tripper," "If I Needed Someone," and "I'm Down." Although cameras were present, they stopped rolling for The Beatles' numbers because of a contractual dispute, so no footage exists of this milestone event.

Left: The Beatles rehearsing at BBC Television Centre for what was their only appearance on *Top of the Pops*. They perform the new single, "Paperback Writer," and the B-side, "Rain," which had been released six days earlier. Both songs had innovative features. As far as "Paperback Writer" was concerned, it was neither a love song nor a dance number, and featured Paul playing what amounted to lead bass. On "Rain" there was the distinctive sound of the backwards guitar. Some critics thought the group's bubble had burst, but the fans still made the single their tenth No. 1 success.

Back to Germany

The Beatles leave for a four-day tour of
Germany, their first visit to the country since
the final trip to Hamburg in December 1962.

Tokyo

After Germany The Beatles fly to
Tokyo, where they perform at
the Budokan Hall. The authorities
went to great lengths to confine
Beatlemania to the concert venue,
and even inside the auditorium the
fans were strictly marshaled. This
made for an unusual situation at
a Beatles concert: the band could
actually be heard. The flaws in the
group's singing and playing—the
result of several years of deafening
noise drowning out the music—
were exposed on this occasion.
Whether the fans noticed or cared is
another matter.

Facing the music

The group arrive back in London and hold a Press conference, following their fraught trip to the Far East. If the Japan leg of the tour had had its difficulties, they were nothing compared with what was to come in the Philippines. A mix-up meant the four missed an appointment to meet the country's First Lady, Imelda Marcos. This was taken as a direct snub, and The Beatles found themselves in the extraordinary situation of being the focal point of a country's vitriol instead of hero-worship. They and their entourage were involved in some ugly scenes of intimidation and assault before managing to get airborne.

Opposite above: Come home soon; the message from their faithful fans as The Beatles fly off to the United States.

Opposite below left: There is a delay in the flight which is to take the group to the United States for their final tour. To kill time they are shown round the new police station at London Airport.

The flight finally gets away, with the usual rousing accompaniment. The reception at the other end is less certain, as John's remarks on the relative popularity of The Beatles and Jesus are rehashed and misquoted. Bonfires are held to burn Beatles records and merchandise, before John eats a little humble pie and manages to smooth things over. In Canada, meanwhile, John has at least one ally in the shape of the Bishop of Montreal, the Rt. Rev. Kenneth Maguire, who said: "I wouldn't be surprised if The Beatles actually were more popular than Jesus. In the only popularity poll in Jesus's time he came out second best to Barabbas."

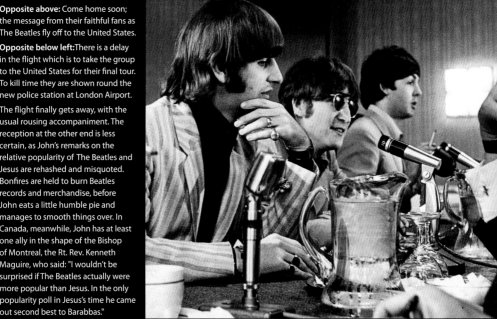

The show is over

Opposite: The fans don't realize it yet, but John, Paul, George, and Ringo knew this was the end of the line as far as touring and concert performance was concerned.

Above left: Just five days after returning from the final US tour, John heads off to Germany for location shooting in Dick Lester's black comedy *How I Won The War*. John has his hair shorn and dons glasses for his role as Private Gripweed.

Right: Paul and Ringo, pictured with Dusty Springfield and Tom Jones at the *Melody Maker* Awards ceremony, held at the top of the GPO Tower, London.

Above right: George at London Airport to meet sitar virtuoso Ravi Shankar, who has been teaching him to play the instrument. George was immersing himself more and more in Indian culture, philosophy, and religion, as well as music, and had just returned from a five-week visit to the country. He was also keen to introduce the sitar into Beatles music, and it had already featured on their albums *Rubber Soul* and *Revolver*.

Not only ... But Also

The Beatles are in the middle of recording "Strawberry Fields Forever," when John makes a guest appearance in a sketch for the Peter Cook and Dudley Moore Christmas show, *Not Only... But Also*. John plays the commissionaire of a "members only" gents lavatory. The outside shots were filmed in Broadwick Street, London, W1.

GENTLEMEN

MEMBERS ONLY

CHAPTER FIVE

1967
Magical Mystery Tour

With no more touring to be done, The Beatles now needed to find a new focus for their lives. On the business front the group had formed The Beatles & Co., a legal partnership to handle all their business affairs that bound them together until 1977, but on a personal level each was looking in a different direction. George was already interested in India and its religions and music, and his passion for this grew and developed throughout the year. Ringo, who was always perhaps more home-loving than the others, began to spend extra time with his family. John tried acting, but decided he didn't like it or the company of most actors. Paul wrote some music for a movie and tried a bit of painting.

Despite these different interests, they still wanted to be together to make music so they turned to the recording studio in earnest, working on their next LP, *Sgt Pepper's Lonely Hearts Club Band*. For some time they had all been experimenting with drugs, including LSD, which had a marked effect on their songwriting—in particular on John's work. The Lennon/McCartney partnership was no longer really a partnership at all, as each was developing his skill in a different way; John was becoming rather introspective and wrote psychedelic and rather disorientating lyrics, while Paul's songs were much more bright and breezy.

The drugs also had another unexpected side-effect. Until now The Beatles public "loveable mop-top" image had more or less survived against the odds, but "A Day In The Life" from *Sgt Pepper* was the first Beatles song to be banned by the BBC, because of its supposed drug references. A couple of days later, when Paul admitted in the newspapers and on television that he had taken LSD, journalists jumped to condemn him. The band's stand on drugs was confirmed when all four Beatles, as well as Brian Epstein, signed a petition published in *The Times* calling for the legalization of marijuana. All this may have disgraced them in the eyes of parents and journalists, but to The Beatles' own generation it just added to their credibility.

But The Beatles themselves were still searching for the Meaning of Life and—having already decided that they were not the answer—had begun to give up drugs. It was at this point that they were introduced to the Maharishi Mahesh Yogi during his visit to London, by George's wife, Pattie. They all initially thought they had found what they were looking for, and threw themselves behind his movement. All four Beatles, as well as many other major pop stars, followed the Maharishi to Bangor in Wales to study transcendental meditation. The Press initially thought this was some sort of publicity stunt, but The Beatles soon made it clear that they were in earnest.

While they were in Wales, the news came of Brian Epstein's accidental death from an overdose of sleeping tablets. He was apparently rich, successful, and happy, but behind the public façade he had felt increasingly lost and depressed after The Beatles gave up touring, since they no longer needed him as much. Despite their rather laid-back public response to the news, they were all devastated. John, in particular, felt that without a manager to lead and organize them, they were finished. At an emergency meeting held at Paul's house days after Brian's death, they discussed their future. Paul suggested they should try to cope by starting work on a project that had been postponed for some time: the filming of the *Magical Mystery Tour*.

The basis of this project was that they should all pile into a bus with a movie crew and various other passengers, and just drive round England filming the adventures they were sure to have. There was no firm script, no experienced director and no one had any idea what they were doing.

They spent a week driving round Cornwall, Devon, and the South of England, followed by photographers and journalists and causing chaos wherever they went, and a further week at West Malling Air Station—since no one had thought to book Shepperton Studios. The resulting ten hours of movie, which took eleven weeks to edit down into the final one-hour version, was shown on BBC television at Christmas and was savagely criticized. The only good news was the music, six new songs written for the movie that were also issued on a pair of EPs in a gatefold sleeve, with a 24-page booklet telling the story in photographs.

Perhaps the critics at the time did not make enough allowances for the experimental nature of the movie, but by the time it was released The Beatles had moved on anyway. They now saw themselves as businessmen, building an empire in which they would be in total control. The first manifestation of this, the Apple Boutique, opened on Baker Street at the beginning of December.

Previous spread: At the photocall for the *Our World* TV broadcast, it is already evident from their different dress styles that each of The Beatles is developing as an individual.

Left: Paul greets Jane Asher at London Airport.

Opposite: Paul pictured at Heathrow after attending Jane Asher's 21st birthday party in Denver, Colorado. Stripes are in, but this is one Beatle mustache that's living on borrowed time.

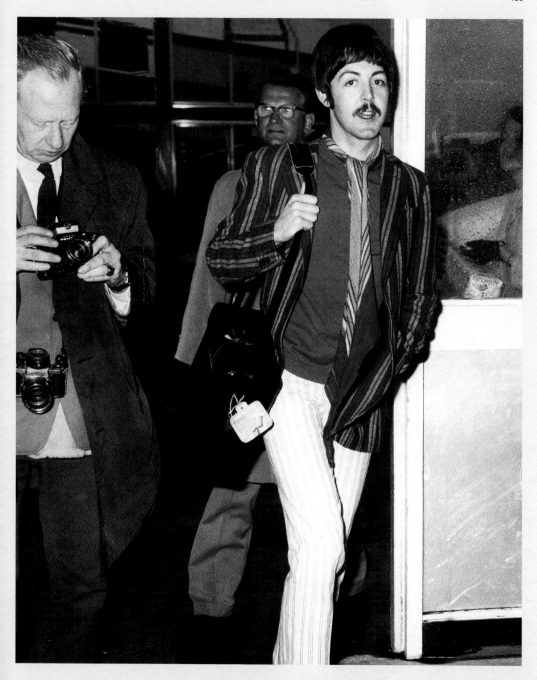

All You Need is Love

A photo-call at Abbey Road Studios in advance of the following day's *Our World* satellite broadcast, in which the group will perform a new song to 400,000,000 people across five continents. For the sake of the global audience, the brief for the song is simplicity. John's response is "All You Need Is Love," composed just days earlier. The song receives both critical and popular acclaim, tops the charts one week after release and becomes the anthem for the "summer of love." The scale of the *Our World* event is fitting, as it marks The Beatles' last live television performance.

Vacation time

Ringo heads off to Athens for a break with the Harrisons, wife Maureen remaining at home, heavily
pregnant with their second child. It was around this time that The Beatles entered into serious
negotiations to buy a Greek island haven for themselves, where they could escape the endless intrusions
on their privacy. The group were to pull out of the deal at the last minute after Greek officials try to use it
for publicity and propaganda purposes.

Above: Paul and John return home from Greece.

Opposite: Paul with Jane Asher and four-year-old Julian Lennon.

Proud Dad

Ringo, with camera at the ready, arrives at Queen Charlotte's Hospital to visit Maureen and new baby son Jason, who was born the previous day.

Opposite above: Ringo and mother-in-law, Mrs Florence Cox. As Zak was named by Ringo, a fan of Western movies, Maureen claims her turn by naming the new arrival—after the Greek mythological hero.

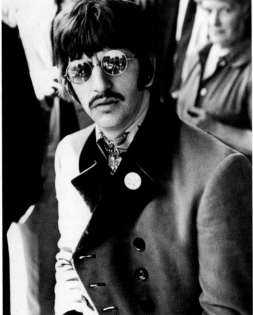

Above and left: The Beatles become interested in transcendental meditation after attending a lecture by the Maharishi Mahesh Yogi in London.

The Maharishi is going on to hold a conference in Wales, and all The Beatles decide to attend. Ironically, what is intended as a spiritual retreat turns into a scrum involving media and fans as news of the trip leaks out.

Opposite below left: Paul at Euston Station, preparing to leave for Bangor, North Wales, where the conference on transcendental meditation is being held.

Opposite above: John's £1000 floral make-over of his Rolls-Royce causes quite a stir. The Phantom V had been black, oozing Establishment, sobriety, and respectability. Six weeks at Fallon's coachworks company, Chertsey, puts a stop to all that.

Opposite below right: Paul at Newquay during the filming of the *Magical Mystery Tour*.

Taking them away—
the Magical Mystery Tour

Above: No mystery here: the bus is simply too wide for the narrow Devon bridge and becomes well and truly stuck. It is an inauspicious start for the *Magical Mystery Tour*, Paul's pet project, conceived back in April, for a movie with no form or script. It is September before shooting starts, a matter of days after Brian Epstein's death.

Opposite: On location in the West Country. Widecombe Fair and Newquay are among the stop-off points on the *Magical Mystery Tour*.

Left and overleaf: Paul and George pictured at the memorial service to Brian Epstein, held on October 17 at the New London Synagogue, Abbey Road.

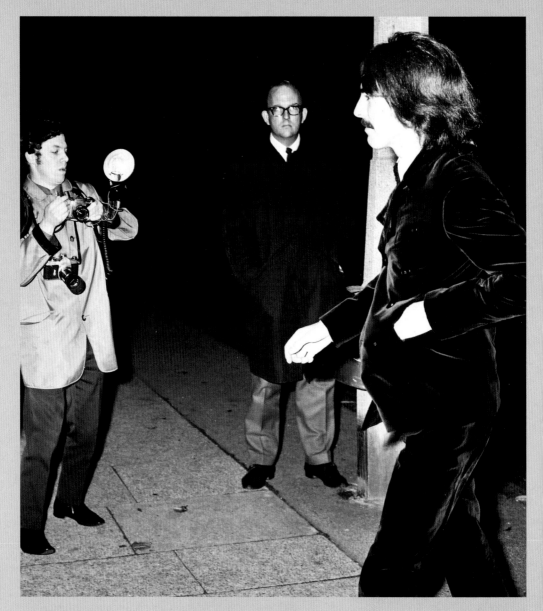

How I Won The War

The day after Epstein's memorial service, Paul, George, and Ringo, with partners and friends, attend the première of *How I Won The War* at the London Pavilion.

Opposite below: John and Cynthia join the other Beatles for a front row view.

Ringo Sweet as Candy

Ringo looks to further his solo acting career
by taking a minor part in the movie *Candy*.
Swedish beauty queen Ewa Aulin plays the
nymphette of the title role.

Above: The director, Christian Marquand,
shows Ringo how to look like a sex-mad
Mexican gardener.

A Psychedelic Garden of Eden

Opposite and left: The Apple Boutique is described as "a psychedelic Garden of Eden for lovers of hippy gear and all the trappings of beautiful living." London's "Beautiful People" certainly turn out for the shop-warming party, but the public stay away in droves.

Above: The Lennons and the Harrisons arriving at the Apple Boutique, Baker Street, the first venture of their company which bears the same name.

CHAPTER SIX

1968

With A Little Help From My Friends

At the beginning of February, all four Beatles and their partners flew out to India to attend a three-month course in transcendental meditation at the Himalayan retreat of the Maharishi Mahesh Yogi. Ringo and Maureen had had enough after less than two weeks; the spicy vegetarian food did not agree with them and nor did the regime of chanting, meditation, and mass praying. Paul and Jane stayed for only five weeks, but he claimed on his return that the trip had been a success and had done him good. The others left after nearly two months, when they heard rumors that the Maharishi had tried to enlighten some of the female members on the course in a physical rather than a spiritual way—although this later turned out to be just malicious gossip. George continued to pursue his interest in Indian culture and the Hindu religion, but the Maharishi was now out of the picture for good.

The Beatles turned their attention back to business, announcing the formation of Apple Corps Ltd. The plan was that Apple would have several divisions covering such areas as music, movies, electronics, merchandise, and the arts, and one of its functions was to provide creative people with funds to get them started—not in a philanthropic way, but as a business investment. It was a great idea in theory and Paul and John took it very seriously and went into the office regularly to direct operations. However, there was no one to organize everything on a proper business footing and to question if the funds going out would bring back any sort of return. The company soon became a source of easy money to every self-styled innovator, artist, or hippy who happened to come through the door—and also to some Apple executives and staff, who had lavish salaries, bought cars on their expense accounts and made the long lunch into an art form. It was some time before The Beatles realized what was happening and tried to take action.

Meanwhile a new Beatles movie was ready for release: *Yellow Submarine*, a full-length animated feature movie that had been two years in the making. It was based on one of The Beatles' earlier songs and they were consulted at the beginning, but they were not involved in working out the final concept or in developing the storyline. Even the voice-overs were spoken by actors, although the band did write a few new songs, as well as filming a short cameo appearance which was inserted near the end. The movie did not do very good business in Britain because of poor distribution, but it went down very well in America and was highly regarded by the critics, often being referred to as "the best movie The Beatles never made."

John attended the première accompanied by Yoko Ono. He had first met her two years previously and soon felt he had discovered a kindred spirit. In May of 1968 he invited Yoko to his home while Cynthia and Julian were on vacation and from that moment they were inseparable; by the end of 1968 Cynthia and John were divorced. Another Beatles romance had also hit the rocks: although they had announced their engagement the previous Christmas, Paul and Jane Asher had split up for good by July—partly because of his growing friendship with American photographer Linda Eastman.

Throughout this period the group had been in the studio working on their double LP, *The Beatles*—which soon commonly became known as the *White Album* to distinguish it from the name of the band. One unexpected advantage of their long stay in India was that it had removed them from their usual surroundings and provided an ideal environment in which to develop their music. When they came back, both John and Paul had written quite a few songs and there were now enough for the new album. Unfortunately it was not long before problems surfaced. The Beatles were now much less a group and more four individuals, each intent on doing his own thing. Paul and

John did not really like each other's new songs, and George felt that his were being dismissed. On top of this, Yoko was soon ever-present in the studio, sitting next to John and whispering suggestions into his ear, encouraging him in his most extreme and avant-garde ideas. The other three bitterly resented her presence, as until then no outsiders had been allowed in the recording studio itself when they were working—even wives and girlfriends had only been welcome to watch from the control room. Meanwhile, Ringo was becoming increasingly unhappy with his role in the group. He could be ignored for hours at a time as the others worked out the words and harmonies of a song, and after criticism of his drumming one day, he walked out. He was soon persuaded to return, but deeper problems remained and this was the beginning of the end of The Beatles.

Below: Bring in the clown; George and John sample Apple's hospitality.
Previous spread: John and Yoko with balloons, at the opening of his exhibition, "You Are Here."

George before and after his trip to India. He had just completed his first movie score, composing and producing the soundtrack for the movie *Wonderwall*.

We've got to hide ourselves away...

Above: New four-piece band Grapefruit must have hoped for even a fraction of the success of the pop luminaries ranged behind them (l to r: Brian Jones, Donovan, Ringo, John, Cilla Black, Paul). The occasion was a Press reception at the Hanover Grand, London, to mark the launch of the group's debut single "Dear Delilah." The band, who had been discovered by head of Apple Terry Doran, would make little impact on the charts, however. "Dear Delilah" peaked at No 21, while their only other chart entry was "C'mon Marianne," which reached No. 31.

Left: John, Cynthia, and George at the Revolution Club, Mayfair, for a fashion show in which Pattie takes to the catwalk. Next to John is Alexis Mardas, otherwise known as Magic Alex, Apple's electronics wizard.

Opposite above: Paul and fiancée Jane Asher head off with Ringo and Maureen to the Maharishi's private residence in India. The Lennons and Harrisons had left a few days earlier. They were looking forward to "locking themselves away" from the world for a while, according to Paul.

Opposite below: Paul and Jane arrive back in London after five weeks in India.

The Big Apple

Where else could John and Paul announce the founding of the Apple Corps but in New York? The philosophy behind the Apple organization was to help others to help themselves; a lot of people soon take the idea literally—helping themselves to Apple's resources. A client list that includes James Taylor and Mary Hopkin—as well as The Beatles themselves—ensures that Apple Records is profitable from the beginning; other branches of the corporation soon degenerate into chaos and financial disaster.

The Beatles return five days later, each brandishing the symbol of the newly-formed empire.

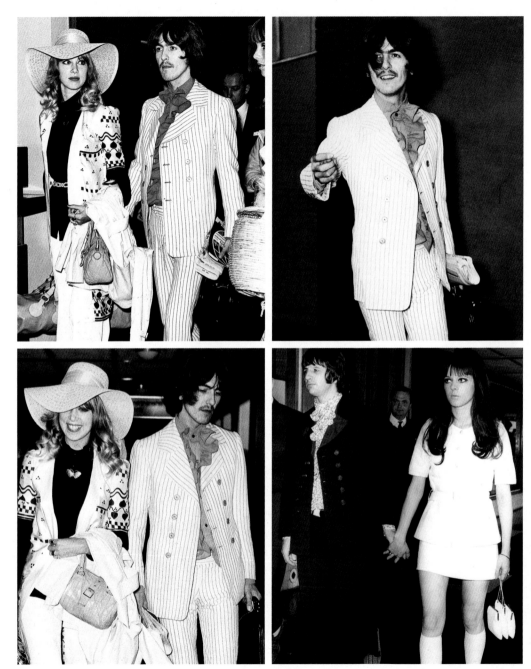

In his Own Write

Opposite and left: The Harrisons and the Starrs fly to the Cannes Film Festival. Although the destination is France, George's spiritual home is still India; his interest in the religion, culture, and music of the country will endure.

At this time Ringo reveals that his diffidence about his own acting talent led him to reject several starring roles—including playing Dr. Watson in a Sherlock Holmes movie—choosing instead the minor part of the gardener in *Candy*.

Below: John and Yoko at the National Theatre for the first night of *In His Own Write*, a play adapted from two of Lennon's books and based loosely on his own childhood. With John and Yoko is the play's co-producer, Victor Spinetti.

I Love You...

John goes back to his art college roots; he holds an exhibition at the

Hey Jude

It's like Beatlemania all over again as the group attend the London première of *Yellow Submarine*. Apart from the soundtrack, The Beatles' contribution to the movie is minimal; they did not even select the song on which the animated feature would be based.

Opposite above left: Paul at his father's Wirral home, on the day after it is announced that his five-year-long relationship with Jane Asher is over.

Opposite above right: Paul with Apple recording artist Mary Hopkin. Her song "Those Were The Days" tops the charts for six weeks in the fall of '68. The song which it knocks off the top spot is "Hey Jude"—which had spent just two weeks at No. 1.

Opposite below: Gear change. Madame Tussaud's employee Juliet Simpkins checks the detail on the latest Beatle outfits. This is the Fab Four's fifth fashion update—at a total cost of £1000—since they were first exhibited in 1964.

No more drugs

Right and opposite below left: John and Yoko have now become inseparable, with Yoko even attending recording sessions. Her influence is already placing a strain on the group. Ringo actually quits The Beatles for a short time during the making of the *White Album*, but this is hushed up and he is later persuaded to return.

Below: In October John and Yoko are charged with possession of cannabis at Marylebone Court and remanded on bail until November 28.

Opposite above: John claims his drug-taking days are over as he is fined £150 for possession of cannabis. The charges against Yoko are dropped.

Opposite below right: Five-year-old Julian Lennon gets to see a circus with a difference: a rehearsal of *The Rolling Stones' Rock And Roll Circus*, featuring a host of stars performing circus and variety acts. John himself is down to do a spot of juggling, but the show never reaches the screen.

CHAPTER SEVEN

1969

All You Need Is Love

Their records were still outstandingly successful, but all four of The Beatles privately knew that as a group they were in trouble. Of them all, Paul was the most committed to keeping the band together and he also missed performing live in front of an audience. He reasoned that the main differences from the old days were that they no longer played together as a group and, because of spending weeks overlaying extra parts, took forever to record each song. He decided that the solution lay in a return to performing live again and he tried to persuade the others to agree. Touring was definitely out, but they reluctantly decided to prepare for a concert or a television broadcast—with rehearsals being filmed for a documentary provisionally entitled *Get Back*, which was finally released as *Let It Be*.

The Beatles assembled at Twickenham Studios at the beginning of January, but almost immediately tensions within the group surfaced again, and this time it was George who walked out. He was persuaded to return, but the idea of doing a concert was shelved and they moved to their new Abbey Road recording studio to concentrate on making an LP. Keyboard player Billy Preston was invited to join them, which defused some of the tension and the recording proceeded. At the end of January, the group even played a live concert out of sight on the roof of the Apple building, which was filmed

as part of the documentary. However, the finished tapes for the LP itself sounded so bad that The Beatles decided not to release it for the moment and went back to the studio to start again. Perhaps everyone knew it was the end, but this time they were all on their best behavior and the result was *Abbey Road*, one of their finest LPs.

At the beginning of 1969, the group had also realized that they needed to do something about Apple Corps Ltd., which had been losing money hand over fist ever since it was formed. However, they disagreed on who should be put in control to set matters straight. John and Yoko wanted Allen Klein, a tough New Yorker who was already involved in the music business, and they convinced George and Ringo to join them in appointing his company, ABKCO, to sort out Apple. But Paul didn't trust Klein and wanted instead the New York firm of Eastman & Eastman—run by his girlfriend Linda's father and brother. The others felt the Eastmans would just be looking out for Paul's best interests, so although they were appointed as general counsel it was under Klein. The band had never done anything before that was not unanimously agreed, but this time Paul was outvoted.

As well as Apple, there were other major problems in their business affairs that came to a head in 1969. The Beatles lost their controlling interest in Brian Epstein's old company, NEMS, and in Northern Songs, the company which published their songs. This meant that they no longer owned the rights to any of their compositions, so valuable publishing royalties were now going to other people and other companies. Klein failed in his attempt to stop this happening, but he did manage to secure a vastly improved royalty deal from EMI for the group's American sales, which even impressed Paul.

Each of The Beatles was now developing an individual career. George had already released a solo album and was getting involved in projects with other artistes, while Ringo was developing his acting career by co-starring in *The Magic Christian*, a movie with Peter Sellers, and also working on his first solo album. Paul had started on his album, *McCartney*, and he also got married at last, to Linda Eastman. John and Yoko had finally been able to marry and now began to give free rein to even their most outlandish ideas, including two "bed-ins" for peace and appearing in public shrouded in large white bags. They also released avant-garde recordings by The Plastic Ono Band

and produced movies attempting to portray themselves spiritually rather than physically, all of which caused much adverse comment in the Press. John was now often absent when the others were recording Beatles numbers, but they just carried on without him.

Paul was still trying to keep the group together, but was fighting a losing battle. John had already told Allen Klein that he wanted to leave The Beatles, but had been persuaded not to say anything to anyone else since negotiations with EMI were at a delicate stage. However, when Paul started pushing again for them to do a series of live performances, John announced his intentions to the others as well. They all agreed to keep it quiet for the moment, so as far as the public were concerned everything was continuing as normal—whereas in fact Paul was now the only one who still wanted to be a Beatle.

Previous spread: Alone at last; Paul and Linda off on honeymoon.
Below: John and Yoko at a Press conference following a trip to Vienna.
Opposite: Filming the studio sessions for *Let It Be*.

Paul to marry?

Opposite above: The rumor-mill is in overdrive concerning the last bachelor Beatle. Paul's name is linked with American photographer Linda Eastman, a 25-year-old divorcee with a six-year-old daughter.

Opposite below: Linda Eastman takes flak from Paul's adoring female fans as the couple leave the Apple building in Paul's Mini. Paul has jettisoned the Castro-style beard which he sported for the celebrated Apple rooftop session a week earlier.

Above: The buck stops here. George declares an end to extravagant charitable giving. It follows a statement from John that they would all be broke in six months if the Apple Corporation continued hemorrhaging money at the present rate.

Left: Paul rehearses for the documentary which was released as *Let It Be*.

It's official

Opposite: Paul and Linda at a launch party for Apple recording artist Mary Hopkin's debut album, held at the GPO Tower. The album had been produced by Paul.

On March 11 the rumors are proved to be true; Marylebone Register Office is booked for the following morning. Laid-back Paul buys the wedding ring which cost £12 "just before the shop shut."

By Beatles' standards it is a quiet affair. There are no guests, and outside the register office photographers easily outnumber the assembled fans. Predictably, those who do turn up are mostly female and mostly distraught. Even so, Paul and Linda play safe and enter the building by a side door—past the trash cans (*above*).

At last...

Paul's best man is brother Mike McGear, of Scaffold fame, reversing their roles of the previous year, when Paul did the honors at Mike's wedding. Two hours after the register office ceremony, Paul and Linda have their marriage blessed by the Rev. Noel Perry-Gore, at St. John's Wood Parish Church.

Linda takes the opportunity to scotch Press reports that she is an heiress with family connections to Eastman-Kodak. "I've been done, where's the money," quips Paul.

Following the wedding, however, it is business as usual; the McCartneys have no immediate honeymoon plans and Paul gets straight back to work.

George and Pattie drugs charge

George and Pattie are remanded on bail for cannabis possession at Esher and Walton Magistrates' Court, and are later fined £250 each.

John and Yoko's turn to marry

Opposite: Just eight days after Paul and Linda's wedding, John and Yoko Ono marry secretly in Gibraltar, then stage a very public "bed-in" at the Amsterdam Hilton. "Stay in bed, grow your hair" is the couple's anti-violence, anti-war message.

Left and below: John and Yoko returning from Vienna on April 1, where they saw the world première of *Rape*, their controversial production whose aim was to analyse the effect of blanket, intrusive TV coverage on an individual's life. In it, a girl is relentlessly pursued by a camera crew, who invade her life but refuse to speak to her.

The Magic Christian

Left: Ringo plays Peter Sellers' son in Terry Southern's satire *The Magic Christian*. The movie's soundtrack features a McCartney song, "Come And Get It," performed by Badfinger, a group signed to Apple.

Opposite: Ringo and Peter Sellers throw their money around at a party celebrating the end of shooting. Each of the 300 guests invited to the Mayfair gaming club was given $1 million on arrival—but the faces on the notes bore an uncanny resemblance to Messrs Starr and Sellers and the money was valid only in the club casino.

Above: Paul leaving the Apple offices, following yet another meeting regarding the troubled corporation's finances. The rift between the members of the group widens as Paul wants to bring in New York law firm Eastman and Eastman—Linda's father and brother. The others are suspicious and favor American businessman Allen Klein. Paul is outvoted, bitterly resenting the accusation of nepotism.

The Ballad of John and Yoko

Below: Five-year-old Kyoko Cox, Yoko's daughter by her previous marriage, flies in from New York on her own, to be met by her mother and famous new step-father. Meanwhile, Yoko makes her mark on the charts. The Beatles take "The Ballad of John and Yoko" to No. 1 in June; in the same month she and John record "Give Peace A Chance," with a group of ad hoc musicians, The Plastic Ono Band. It reaches No. 2.

Right: Yoko in her residence at Tittenhurst Park, a 60-acre estate with a mansion near Ascot.

Opposite above right: Ringo makes sure his latest release gets into shot as he takes a break after the movie is completed. Working on *The Magic Christian* had been a respite from the troubled Beatles' recording sessions, in which Ringo sometimes found himself sidelined, with Paul taking over on drums.

Opposite above left: George returning from a vacation in Sardinia. Like Ringo before him, George had actually quit The Beatles earlier in the year, following studio disagreements. Although he too returned a few days later, the cracks were now becoming impossible to paper over.

Opposite below: Paul and Linda at the première of the movie *Alfred The Great*.

Kindred Spirits

George finds a group of kindred spirits at London's Radha Krishna Temple, a Hindu sect which trains people in the process of self-purification. Members of Radha Krishna Temple shave their heads and ban drugs, alcohol and "sex without children." The "Hare Krishna Mantra" becomes the unlikeliest pop hit of the year, peaking at No. 12.

Opposite below: Just fans, like everybody else. John, George, and Ringo, with spouses, are faces in a 150,000-strong crowd, all of whom have come to see Bob Dylan perform at the Isle of Wight pop festival in September.

CHAPTER EIGHT

1970
Revolution

At the beginning of 1970, John and Yoko hit the headlines again. An exhibition of John's lithographs at the London Arts Gallery was raided by the police and eight erotic pictures depicting him and Yoko on their honeymoon were confiscated. John had also been taking heroin regularly and early in the year he entered a clinic to be cured of his addiction. Ringo's movie, *The Magic Christian*, had its première in New York in February and although the movie did not do well, his performance was complimented. He also released his LP, *Sentimental Journey*, which was not well received by the critics but did briefly enter the American charts. George was working on his new LP, *All Things Must Pass*, and Paul was putting the finishing touches to his first album, *McCartney*.

All The Beatles' contractual affairs were in a mess, and Allen Klein discovered that, despite what they had been led to believe, *Yellow Submarine* did not constitute the third in their three-movie contract with United Artists. However, there had been enough material filmed for *Get Back*, their proposed television documentary, to turn it into a full-length feature movie instead—which they could sell to UA. There was also the LP recorded at the same time, which had not been released due to its poor quality. None of The Beatles wanted to have anything more to do with this, so Allen Klein appointed American producer Phil Spector to

try to make something of it. His trademark was a dramatic, heavily orchestrated "wall of sound" that had been used to great effect on other artistes' songs, but which was in total contrast to the way The Beatles normally recorded.

When the LP was ready for release, Paul was horrified to discover what had been done to it and in particular that his song "The Long And Winding Road" had been almost swamped by the addition of a full orchestra and a female choir. He insisted that his original version was restored, but both Klein and the other Beatles ignored his protests. They also tried to delay the planned release of *McCartney*, so that it would not clash with the release of the Beatles LP and movie, both now retitled *Let It Be* after one of Paul's songs. It was all too much, and in the press release that went out with advance copies of *McCartney*, Paul said that he had no plans to work with The Beatles again, and that he had not missed them while making his new LP. This was taken as an announcement that he was leaving The Beatles and the news prompted headlines in newspapers all round the world. The irony was that although Paul had been the first to say anything publicly, he was the last to make the decision that The Beatles were finished.

The movie and LP *Let It Be* were released just afterward, and the LP shot up the charts on a wave of nostalgia—even though most critics decided it was poor in quality and by no means showed The Beatles at their best. "The Long And Winding Road" was also released as a single in America at the same time, and despite Paul's reservations went straight to No. 1. *McCartney* was an international success, as was George's LP, *All Things Must Pass*. John's single, "Instant Karma," had been a big hit earlier in the year and his LP, *John Lennon/The Plastic Ono Band*, went into the top twenty. Only Ringo was not doing so well, with his second LP, *Beaucoups of Blues*, getting a positive reception but only just making it into the charts. However, his best was yet to come.

Although The Beatles as a group were officially no more, with each member set on a solo career, the business side of things was by no means easy to resolve. The four of them were still legally tied together until 1977 by The Beatles & Co., the company they had formed three years earlier. Under the terms of their agreement, all the income that any of them made, even from their solo albums, was to be split four ways. In addition, Paul remained unhappy about Allen Klein's involvement in his affairs, even more so after he realized that Klein had pocketed around £5m in his first year of handling The Beatles. He had also been told by the Eastmans of the rumors about Klein in America, where quite a few lawsuits had been filed against him and where his business methods were well known. He couldn't just opt out of the agreement with the other Beatles so the only way out for him was to dissolve the partnership. At the end of December he filed a lawsuit in London seeking a dissolution of The Beatles & Co. and the appointment of a receiver to sort out the band's affairs.

Previous spread: Ringo and Maureen arriving back from the US première of *The Magic Christian* in New York.

Left: George with Ravi Shankar at the start of an Indian Arts Season at the Royal Festival Hall.

Going solo

The mood within The Beatles is now firmly on individual projects; After *The Magic Christian* Ringo turns his attention to a solo album, *Sentimental Journey*. Even Paul has finally accepted that the break-up of The Beatles is irrevocable.

Above: Paul had begun recording tracks for his own solo album, *McCartney*, at the end of '69. This creates even more friction, as Allen Klein and the other members of the group try to prevent its release clashing with *Let It Be*.

All Things Must Pass

George renews his friendship with Ravi Shankar (*overleaf*) during an Indian Arts Season, held at the Royal Festival Hall in September. On the musical front, George enlists Phil Spector to produce his first solo project, the ambitious triple album *All Thing Must Pass*. They spend six months in the studio—compared to the six days Ringo spent making *Beaucoups of Blues*. It is well received by critics, and the record-breaking cover price does not deter the fans.

Opposite: Paul and Linda, looking serenely happy as news of The Beatles' split reverberates round the world.

Opposite: John and Yoko pictured in November, just prior to the release of the album *John Lennon/The Plastic Ono Band*, which reaches No. 11 in the charts. It was around this time that Paul wrote to John on the subject of the dissolution of Apple. John replied with a postcard which read: "Get well soon. Get the other signatures and I'll think about it." It was responses such as these which precipitated Paul's decision to sue.

Below: George with Ravi Shankar.

CHAPTER NINE

1971

You Never Give Me Your Money

The High Court case to dissolve The Beatles' company was heard in London during February and March and Paul was the only Beatle to attend, supported by his wife, Linda. The others still believed that Allen Klein was their savior so they felt that Paul was merely out to cause trouble. At the time he was also disliked by many fans and was having a hard time in the Press because they all blamed him for breaking up the group. He claimed he was not going through the court case just for himself, but for all the Beatles, since their entire empire was about to vanish into someone else's pocket. His counsel pointed out that Paul would actually be better off sticking to the terms of the original agreement, since the most successful record of that financial year had been George's single, "My Sweet Lord," which had become the best-selling single of 1971. However, it soon became apparent that Allen Klein had taken at least $500,000 more than he was entitled to on The Beatles' American royalty deal, and the High Court judge finally ruled in favor of Paul. The other three Beatles were furious, but at the same time felt a sense of release—now they were really free to pursue individual careers.

George was initially riding high, with both his last LP and his latest single at the top of the charts. Unfortunately an American music publisher then claimed that "My Sweet Lord" plagiarized a hit of the 1960s, "He's So Fine," by the Chiffons. The court battles were to go on for years, before George was defeated and had to pay out thousands of dollars. Meanwhile his interest in India led him to organize *Concert For Bangladesh*, two concerts at Madison Square Garden in New York in aid of famine victims. The first was of Indian music specially composed by Ravi Shankar and the second boasted an all-star line-up, all performing for free, including George, Ringo, Bob Dylan, and Eric Clapton. The concerts, with an accompanying album and movie, raised an enormous amount, well over $10m. Unfortunately a great deal of money was creamed off by the various record companies involved and by the tax authorities—even though all the proceeds were for charity—and only a small percentage of the total actually made it to Bangladesh.

John released one of his most critically acclaimed solo albums, *Imagine*, which topped the charts in both Britain and America. The songs were much more gentle—more commercial and less avant-garde—than those John had released previously, but also included a bitter attack on Paul in a song called "How Do You Sleep?." This was also the year that John was allowed back to America. For several years he had been refused entry because of his drug convictions, but in September 1971 the authorities relented and John and Yoko flew to New York for a short visit, which turned into a permanent stay. The Press in Britain had done nothing but ridicule them and their beliefs and make fun of Yoko as an artist, but in America they were much less critical and seemed more open to new ideas.

Ringo surprised everybody. Since his first two LPs had not been that well received, many people were beginning to think that he would not succeed in a solo career. However, he now released his new single, "It Don't Come Easy," recorded with George and their old friend from Hamburg, Klaus Voormann, and it quickly reached No. 5 on both sides of the Atlantic. He soon proved this wasn't just a flash in the pan either, as he followed it up with three more hit singles and an LP in the following couple of years.

Paul's second solo album, *Ram*, also found critical success, although his catchy songs were much more popular with the fans than with the music Press. Unlike the others, whose albums were all done with new bands, both of Paul's LPs featured only himself, with the odd contribution from Linda. He still missed performing live and he was keen to get out on the road again, so in August he formed his own new band, Wings. The lineup included several accomplished musicians—and also Linda on keyboards even though she was a photographer with little musical skill. The music world was highly critical of her abilities, making fun of her voice and deriding her for appearing to muscle in on Paul's group. It was not the first time Linda had suffered bad Press—general coverage of her had often been critical after their marriage, for very little apparent reason.

But the burning question on everyone's mind seemed to be: would The Beatles ever get back together again? It was the subject of endless speculation in the Press, and each individual Beatle could be sure that he would be asked the question at least once in every Press conference.

Previous spread: John and Yoko on their way to Majorca.

Left: Paul's father, Jim, and stepmother, Mary, join in the celebrations at the launch of Wings.

The long and grinding road

Paul and Linda pictured during the nine-day hearing at the High Court.

Paul reveals that they are soon to depart for France, where he will record a new album featuring just himself and Linda. It is one of the earliest indications that Linda will play a part in Paul's future musical output.

Above: Ringo and Maureen at a farewell party for Peter Sellers, who is about to become a tax exile in Ireland. Tax liability is also one of the central issues in The Beatles' legal wrangle.

Opposite: Paul's second solo album, *Ram*, is about to hit the stores as the Lennons pay a visit to Majorca. Over the summer, John takes to his Tittenhurst Park Studios to record *Imagine*. The personal spat between John and Paul is continued in both the visual and lyrical content of these two albums.

Jagger's Wedding

The McCartneys en route to Mick Jagger and Bianca Perez-Mora's wedding in St. Tropez. The Starrs are also invited to the Jaggers' wedding, which brings Ringo and Paul a little too close for comfort.

Opposite: John at Apple, soon after the release of his single, "Working Class Hero."

It Don't Come Easy

Right: Ringo's "It Don't Come Easy" was riding high in the charts at the time of the trip to Mick Jagger's wedding.

Below: With the release of *Imagine* still several weeks away, Yoko takes center stage with the publication of her book *Grapefruit*. Yoko had published 500 copies of her collection of "instructional poems" some seven years earlier, and had sent John a copy. The content was a series of enigmatic thoughts, such as: "Draw a map to get lost," and "Smoke everything you can, including your pubic hair."

Opposite: Paul and Linda host a gala evening at the Empire Ballroom, Leicester Square, to launch their new group, Wings.

Drummer Denny Siewell and Denny Laine, the ex-Moody Blues guitarist/vocalist, complete the Wings lineup.

CHAPTER TEN

After The Beatles

The Long and Winding Road

For the first few years of the Seventies there was still substantial bad feeling between Paul and the other three former Beatles. Their business affairs took a while to untangle, as Allen Klein and ABKCO did not reach the end of their term as business managers of Apple and the other Beatles companies until the end of March 1973 and The Beatles & Co. partnership was not formally dissolved in the London High Court until January 1975.

Meanwhile, Paul went back to touring with Wings and their music steadily improved. Unfortunately two members of the band quit in August 1973, just before they were due to fly to Lagos, Nigeria, to record their next album. Paul, Linda, and the remaining member, Denny Laine, carried on without them and produced their best album to date, *Band On The Run*. In the next few years Wings had a constantly changing lineup, but their follow-up album, *Venus And Mars*, was equally successful. The world tour made in 1975/76 was a sell-out, and Paul later said he made more money in this period than he ever had with The Beatles.

John and Yoko's friends in New York included a whole crowd of left-wing radicals and political activists and the American government soon took note and began moves to get him deported. John fought the action, but the strain had its effect on his marriage and towards the end of 1973

he left Yoko in New York and went to Los Angeles with their secretary, May Pang. What was supposed to be a temporary separation turned into a fifteen-month "lost weekend," as John settled into a house with Keith Moon and Ringo and the three of them over-indulged in drink and drugs.

Despite this, John managed to produce two good albums, *Walls and Bridges* and *Rock 'n' Roll*, but he still pined for Yoko and finally pulled himself together and returned to her in New York in January 1975. After their son, Sean, was born later in 1975, John announced that he was taking five years off to play with his baby while Yoko carried on working. They settled in New York permanently, since the deportation order against John had finally been lifted and he was granted his Green Card.

Ringo followed up the success of "It Don't Come Easy" with three more hit singles and an LP, *Ringo*, in 1973 on which John, Paul, and George were all featured—although Paul at no point recorded at the same time as John or George. Still, it was the nearest thing to a Beatles reunion so far achieved. His acting career also continued, including what many believe was his best film, *That'll Be The Day*, with David Essex. After this high point, Ringo's musical career began to go downhill. His marriage also hit the rocks, which was when he joined John and Keith Moon on their bender in Los Angeles.

He and Maureen divorced acrimoniously in 1975 and after this Ringo spent much of the remainder of the Seventies wandering round the world, being seen with various foreign girls in various countries and drinking too much.

After having said he would never tour again, George did one tour across America in 1974, which was not a great success; although the concerts were a sell-out, a throat infection had made his voice hoarse. Fans were also angry that he refused to play many Beatles numbers and said his new music was too experimental. He came close to a nervous breakdown afterward—things were not going well in his musical career and his marriage to Pattie was breaking up. George and Pattie divorced in 1977, and in 1978 George married Olivia Arias, whom he had met when she came to work as a secretary at his record company. The wedding had been postponed because of the death of George's father, and was rescheduled after the birth of their first and only child, a boy called Dhani. Toward the end of the Seventies, George became involved in the British film industry when he helped the Monty Python team raise funding for their film, *The Life Of Brian*. Afterward he formed his own production company, HandMade Films, which made quite a few successful films, mainly based on British subjects and locations.

At the end of the Seventies, Paul's doubts about Allen Klein were proved to have been prophetic, when Klein was jailed in America after it was found that there were major irregularities in his accounting for the income he had creamed off George's *Concert for Bangladesh* project. By this time, relations between Paul and the others were much improved. Paul had played with John while visiting Los Angeles in 1973, and Paul, George, and Ringo had reunited for a jam session at the garden party after Eric Clapton's wedding to the former Pattie Harrison in May 1979.

Having completed his promised five years looking after Sean, John returned to recording and brought out a new album, *Double Fantasy*, just in time for his son's fifth birthday in 1980. The reviews were good and John seemed happy and full of enthusiasm in interviews he gave around this time. On December 8, as he came out of the Dakota building where he lived in New York, he was stopped by Mark Chapman and signed a copy of *Double Fantasy* for him. Chapman then waited outside the building all day until John returned from the studio much later that night. He fired five shots at point-blank range and although John was rushed to hospital he was pronounced dead when he arrived.

The sense of grief and outrage at his death was overwhelming all around the world, but was even more hysterical in America. In Britain there had been little news of him over the previous few years and he was regarded as someone who had become a bit eccentric and retired from the cutting edge of music. In America he had captured the hearts of those opposed to the war in Vietnam and his song "Give Peace A Chance" had become their anthem. Many of them felt they had lost an inspirational leader. On December 14 Yoko called for ten minutes of silence to be observed at 7.00pm GMT around the world in his memory and throughout December the airwaves were full of the sound of "Imagine," one of his best-loved songs.

Ringo had recovered from his alcoholism and had met a new partner, American actress Barbara Bach, while filming *Caveman* early in 1980. They were involved in a serious car crash in London the same year, but both escaped without injury. He was badly shaken by John's death and the following year he left America and with Barbara returned to Britain, where they were married in April. After his return he also patched things up with Maureen and became closer to his children, much of whose growing-up he had missed while roaming round the world. His musical career faltered for a while, but he still did some acting and in 1984 he recorded the narration for a series of *Thomas the Tank Engine*, for many children becoming for ever the cheeky voice of Thomas.

Even before John's death, the Eighties began badly for Paul. He had twice been refused permission to tour Japan with Wings because of his previous drug convictions, but finally the Japanese authorities had relented. Arriving in Japan at the beginning of January, Paul was searched by customs men at Narita Airport and they found a large stash of cannabis. He was thrown into prison and the local British Consul warned that they might try to make an example of him with a sentence of several years. Luckily after only eight days he was released and deported back to England. It was the final straw for the remaining members of Wings, and although they continued to record for several further months they had split up for good by the end of the year. Paul went on to release a series of solo albums, but unfortunately also decided to get involved in making another film. He wrote both the songs and the script for *Give My Regards To Broad Street*, which was savagely attacked by the critics and died at the box office.

After John's death, George became even more obsessive about his privacy. Throughout the Eighties he was perhaps best known for his involvement in HandMade Films, although he never used his Beatle persona to promote the pictures they made or attended star-studded premières. He also released a best-selling solo album, *Cloud Nine*, and toured with Roy Orbison, Tom Petty, Jeff Lynne, and Bob Dylan as The Traveling Wilburys. Gardening became one of his overwhelming interests, and he spent a great deal of time and energy growing exotic plants in his 36-acre garden in Oxfordshire.

One unexpected result of John's death was that the other three Beatles started collaborating again. Ringo had always got on well with both Paul and George—and with John before his death—but George and Paul now tried to bury their differences. George's tribute to John, "All Those Years Ago," which was released not long after his death, featured backing by Paul and Ringo. Right back in the Seventies The Beatles had planned to produce a documentary that would tell their story in their own words, tentatively titled *The Long And Winding Road*. The project had suffered the same fate as many others after their break-up—the four of them could never agree on what and how things should be done. Now everyone else who had ever been connected with The Beatles seemed to be bringing out retrospectives and anniversary tributes, and the three remaining Beatles agreed it was perhaps time to have their final say.

The original idea was that this documentary would be a straightforward record telling the true story, since they all felt that everyone else had got it wrong. They started by going back to the archives to see what was there, and were surprised by

Previous spread: Three Beatles and a wedding: Ringo and Barbara get married. **Left:** Ringo and George on stage during the Prince's Trust Rock Concert in June '87.

the amount of material that turned up—forgotten interviews, alternative recordings, unfinished songs, and comic out-takes. Some of the material had already found its way on to bootleg records, but much had just been gathering dust at Abbey or in EMI's storerooms around the world. Gradually the project turned into more than just the story of the group and became a collection of pretty much everything The Beatles had ever done, right back to when they were schoolboys. It ended up being both a television documentary and three double LP/CDs, all entitled *The Beatles Anthology*.

Much of the material could never have been released at the time it was recorded because it was either unfinished, early versions of songs, or spoiled/rejected takes, but such material was now interesting because it showed how things had developed—and was invaluable to fans and to music historians. Paul, George, and Ringo were interviewed specially for the documentary, as were three of The Beatles' intimates: George Martin, their recording engineer, Neil Aspinall, their roadie and general assistant, and press officer Derek Taylor. John was included in the form of old interviews, mainly from his solo days. The most controversial part of the project, however, was the inclusion of two brand-new Beatles songs, which were also released as singles.

For years people had been asking if The Beatles were going to get back together again, and even John's death did not stop them—they just substituted Julian Lennon in the lineup. The answer had always been no, but when Paul, George, and Ringo were collecting material, Yoko had sent them some tapes of John's that included several unfinished songs. This sparked the idea that the remaining Beatles could finish them off, adding further instrumentation and harmony vocals. The approach they took mentally was that John had started the song, but was now going off somewhere and had left them to finish it—which was not so different to how they had sometimes worked in the old days. Many people said it couldn't be done and that the three of them were very ill-advised even to try, but they were determined to prove the doubters wrong.

Toward the end of 1995, amidst the sort of hype and publicity that was reminiscent of The Beatles' heyday in the Sixties, the first single, "Free As A Bird," and the first double LP/CD were released, in conjunction with the television documentary. Newspapers ran whole pages devoted to the "Fab Four" and magazines around the world brought out special editions. The three Beatles themselves did not do much to publicize the project—it was enough that they had set the ball rolling. Even after 25 years The Beatles were still major news—and the new singles did sound like proper Beatles songs, with both going into the top ten in the charts.

During the Nineties, George kept out of the limelight and tended his garden, but when he was stabbed by an intruder at the end of 1999, he received messages of sympathy from all over the world. He had been fighting cancer since 1997 and, despite several operations and experimental radiosurgery, he died at a friend's house in Los Angeles on November 29, 2001. Ringo continued to drum for other artists and has toured America and Europe with his All-Starr Band. This is made up of a variety of featured players—including his son, Zak, who is also an accomplished drummer. Paul continues to record and make live appearances, has tried classical music and animated films and is involved in environmental issues. He received a knighthood in 1997, but soon afterward his wife Linda died

of cancer and he retreated into his private life for a time. He surfaced again to support his daughter, Stella, as she launched her career as a fashion designer and afterwards moved back into the public eye once again. At the end of 1999, when the new Cavern Club in Liverpool was opened, he was the only former Beatle who turned up to play. In July 2001, he became engaged to former model Heather Mills, whom he met through her charity work.

Now both John and George are dead, there can be no more talk of a possible Beatles comeback. But in a way it doesn't matter, because Beatles music is still loved and played around the world, their records are being re-released on CD and no one can ever take away the effect they had on popular music. The group still exists in people's hearts and minds: The Beatles are forever.

Above: Paul during Wings 1989/90 world tour.

Opposite: The full McCartney family arrives at Heathrow; (from l to r) Stella, James with Paul, Mary, Linda, and Linda's daughter Heather.

Back off Boogaloo

Opposite: Maureen, Ringo, Pattie, and George off to the Cannes Film Festival to see the movie of George's *Concert for Bangladesh*.

Ringo's solo career continues in great style, with the release of his second hit single, "Back off Boogaloo." He also directs the filming of T. Rex in concert at the Empire Pool Wembley for *Born to Boogie*, made by Apple Films. Ringo himself appears in the film, in a jam session shot at a recording studio.

Above and right: After spending the first few months of 1972 playing unannounced at universities around Britain, Paul and his band Wings begin their first proper tour with concerts in France, Germany, Switzerland, Denmark, Finland, Sweden, Norway, and the Netherlands. Despite the sniping in the Press, Linda is still an essential part of the lineup.

That'll Be The Day

Ringo looked great in *That'll be the Day* (*below right*), which was set in the late 1950s. It was almost a recreation of his youth, since his character was based in a summer camp similar to the Butlin's camps he had worked in with Rory Storm and the Hurricanes before he joined The Beatles.

After filming had finished Ringo began work on his new LP, *Ringo*, but although things were going well professionally, personally he and Maureen were on the verge of splitting up.

Opposite above left: Paul and Linda during Wings' UK tour.

Opposite below left: "That's my daddy"—Stella joins Paul and Linda at a photo-call.

Opposite above right: Even in the Seventies, Paul and Linda were involved in charitable causes. In November 1973 they made a surprise visit to the Toy For a Sick Child Fund in Piccadilly, where two-year-old Stella donated her teddy, Fruity.

Opposite below right: John in Los Angeles, during his separation from Yoko.

Wings over water...

Below right: Now that all the legal problems of The Beatles break-up were far behind him, Paul seemed more relaxed. He developed a reputation as a family man, spending his free time with Linda and the children.

The McCartneys on the move again, this time off to New Orleans where Paul was recording for his new LP, *Venus and Mars*. Paul had recently met up with John and George in New York, so the Press was full of rumors about The Beatles reforming.

Right: George was going through a bad time during this period. His marriage to Pattie had hit the rocks, and his last LP, *Dark Horse*, had quickly been dubbed "Dark Hoarse" by the critics because of the poor state of his voice.

Below and opposite below: Another tour for Wings, this time their first, and only, tour round the world. The first section began with concerts all round Britain, after which they moved on to Australia.

Opposite above: Linda relaxes during the tour, while Paul entertains Stella and her playmate, Tamsy Lee.

Wings at Wembley

Opposite above and opposite below right:
Wings give two concerts at the Empire Pool,
Wembley, playing to 8,000 people. Two
"journalists" from the USSR also attended one of
the concerts, and Paul announces that he hopes
to tour Russia in the near future.

Opposite below left: Paul attends the première
of *Billy*. Although they were expecting to
have another girl, Paul and Linda's first
son, James Louis, made his appearance on
September 12, 1977.

This page: After his split from Maureen, Ringo
was seen around the world with several different
women, including Nancy Andrews and Shelley
Duvall. At one point he even became engaged
to Nancy, but it was short-lived.

Opposite right and above: To promote their new LP, *London Town*, Wings took the Press on a boat ride down the Thames, with fish and chips to eat. Wings now consisted of Paul, Linda, and Denny Laine, with two session musicians on guitar and drums to make up numbers.

Opposite left: Things were finally looking up for George. He had a new love, Olivia Arias, a new hobby, Grand Prix racing, and a new hairdo, curly. His last LP, *331/3*, had been a critical success and his divorce from Pattie was finally sorted out, leaving him free to move forward. That year Olivia gave birth to their first and only child, a boy who is called Dhani.

Right: George after he ran over his foot with a tractor that he was using in the grounds of his home at Henley, near Oxford.

100 million albums later...

Opposite right: Paul is awarded the first rhodium disk by Norris McWhirter, editor of *The Guinness Book of Records*, for being the most honored man in music. By their reckoning he has written 43 songs which have sold more than a million copies, has 60 gold disks and his sales of 100 million albums and 100 million singles make him the world's most successful recording artist. The award sparks massive debate among musicologists, who claim it should really have gone to one of the classical musicians such as Beethoven or Strauss.

Opposite left: Ringo's last few records had not been successful, but he faced the Press in July 1978 to promote his new single, "Tonight." It was one of the few public appearances he made toward the end of the Seventies—with no film roles to speak of and his records flopping, he withdrew into his private life and refused to give interviews. His health problems also came to a head in April 1979 when he was rushed into hospital in Monte Carlo, close to death. His illness was part of the long-term after-effects of the peritonitis he suffered when he was six, which had led to him going into a coma for ten weeks and then spending over a year in hospital. This time, after a successful operation to remove five feet of intestine, Ringo was soon back on his feet.

Above: Paul faces the Press at the gates of his Sussex farm, fresh from eight days in prison and deportation from Japan after a large stash of cannabis was found in his luggage.

Ringo and Barbara wed

After the trauma of John's murder, the remaining three Beatles and their families are glad to be gathering for a happy event: Ringo's wedding to Barbara Bach in London.

Opposite below left: George and Olivia run a gauntlet of Press photographers as they leave the Register Office after Ringo's wedding.

Right and below right: A celebration party at the Hippodrome night-club before the London première of *Give My Regards to Broad Street* at the Odeon, Leicester Square, is attended by Paul, Linda, Ringo, and Barbara and Olivia Harrison. George can't make the première, because he is in New Zealand attending a literary luncheon to help Derek Taylor—once Brian Epstein's assistant and then The Beatles' Press Officer during their Beatlemania days—promote his new book, *Fifty Years Adrift*.

Below: Ringo, always ready for a party, dresses in gold brocade for a Chelsea Arts Club masked ball with a Venetian carnival theme. Barbara wears an equally extravagant costume with a head-dress of gold roses. That same year, Ringo becomes the first grandfather Beatle when his daughter-in-law, Sarah Starkey, gives birth to a girl, Tatia Jane.

It was 20 years ago today...

Above right: At a massive party to celebrate the 20th anniversary of the official release date of *Sgt Pepper's Lonely Hearts Club Band*, Paul cuts a slice of cake, helped by Linda and artist Peter Blake, who created the cover picture.

Opposite below left: Back on stage again for the Prince's Trust Rock Concert in June '87, George's guests include Ringo, Eric Clapton, Elton John, and Phil Collins.

Above left: As well as supporting Paul in all his public ventures, such as the annual Buddy Holly Week, Linda begins to develop her own career again throughout the Eighties.

Left: Some of Britain's top rock stars, including George and Ringo, gather to play a concert in honor of rock 'n' roll singer Carl Perkins.

Opposite below right: George also appears in Heartbeat '86, a concert at Birmingham's National Exhibition Centre to raise money for a local children's hospital, along with The Electric Light Orchestra and The Moody Blues.

Opposite above right: George Harrison's company, HandMade Films, picks up a fine collection of honors at The London Standard Film Awards in 1986. *My Beautiful Laundrette* takes top place as Best British Picture of the Year, while *A Private Function* receives the award for Best Screen Play as well as the Peter Sellers Comedy Award for Michael Palin's performance. Meanwhile, filming of HandMade's latest venture, *Shanghai Surprise* starring Madonna, is not going so well. George spends some time on the set, both because of the problems and because a documentary about the making of the film is being shot for UK television's Channel Four.

Opposite above left: Paul is always ready to mess about for the camera. Here he is at his Soho office.

On the road again

Paul still loved performing in
public, and at the end of the
Eighties he formed a new
band to back him during a
twelve-month world tour
beginning in July 1989. The
lineup included Linda as
usual, with guitarists Hamish
Stuart and Robbie McIntosh,
drummer Chris Whitten, and
keyboard player Wix. On
tour Paul is the star, with the
others merely a backing band.
Refusing any sponsorship,
Paul dedicated the tour to
Friends of the Earth—which
didn't mean that they
received any profits but did
give them a platform for their
views in the program.

Bottom right: Paul finishes the Eighties with yet another award, a miniature gold copy of his own guitar, presented by the Performing Rights Society for his contribution to pop music. At the lunch held at Claridge's Paul is given a standing ovation by guests, who included violinist Nigel Kennedy, Bee Gees Maurice, and Robin Gibb, Bruce Welch from The Shadows, Chris Rea, and song-writer Tim Rice.

Right: Paul's world tour continues in January 1990 with concerts in Birmingham and London before he and his entourage return to America for another three months. In London Paul appears at Wembley Arena, opening the concert with a stunning show of lasers and film images covering the history of the world over the past 25 years.

Bottom left: While in the US, Paul meets up with Michael Jackson again. There had been rumors that they had fallen out after Jackson bought the rights to all the Lennon-McCartney songs for $47.5 million, but Paul assures everyone that they are still good friends.

Profits from the concert held in Liverpool during Paul's world tour were to be split between seven charities, but the overheads were so enormous that it only just broke even. Paul donated £100,000 of his own money instead.

Below: In 1991, having been a vegetarian for twenty years along with Paul and the rest of the family, Linda works with a major frozen food company in the UK to launch her own range of frozen pre-cooked vegetarian meals.

Chronology

1934

19 Sept Brian Epstein is born in Liverpool

1939

10 Sept Cynthia Powell is born in Blackpool

1940

23 Jun Stuart Sutcliffe is born in Edinburgh, Scotland

7 Jul Ringo Starr is born at the Royal Liverpool Children's Hospital

9 Oct John Lennon is born at the Oxford Street Maternity Hospital, in Liverpool

1941

24 Jan Randolph Peter Best is born in Madras, India

1942

18 Jun Paul McCartney is born at Walton Hospital, Liverpool

1943

25 Feb George Harrison is born at home at 12 Arnold Grove, Wavertree, Liverpool

1957

Mar John forms The Black Jacks skiffle group with Pete Shotton, which is later renamed The Quarry Men

9 Jun The Quarry Men audition for Carroll Levis' *TV Star Search* at Liverpool's Empire Theatre, but fail to qualify

6 Jul Paul meets John for the first time, when he sees The Quarry Men play at St Peter's Church garden fete in Liverpool

20 Jul Paul is invited to join The Quarry Men

7 Aug The Quarry Men perform at the Cavern Club in Liverpool for the first time

18 Oct Paul's debut performance with The Quarry Men, at the New Clubmore Hall, Liverpool. He played lead guitar, but made a mess of his solo and was demoted to rhythm

1958

6 Feb George meets The Quarry Men and is later invited to join them because of his growing skill as a guitarist, although he is younger than the others

15 Jul Julia, John's mother, is killed by a speeding car when crossing the road after leaving his Aunt Mimi's house

1959

25 Mar Ringo joins Rory Storm and the Hurricanes, at that time Merseyside's top band Aug 29 The Quarry Men play at the opening night of the Casbah Club, owned by Pete Best's mother. The group consists of John, Paul, George, and Ken Brown. They still have no drummer

10 Oct Ken Brown quits The Quarry Men

15 Nov As Johnny and the Moondogs, John, Paul, and George make the final audition for Carroll Levis' *TV Star Search* at Liverpool's Empire Theatre

1960

Jan Stuart Sutcliffe, a friend of John at the Art College, joins The Quarry Men as bass player

May The Quarry Men become The Beatals

10 May The Beatals become The Silver Beetles and audition as a backing group for Billy Fury, but instead are booked to tour Scotland as backing for singer Johnny Gentle

20-28 May The Silver Beetles tour Scotland. The group have also changed their own names: "Long John" Lennon, Paul Ramon (McCartney), Carl (George) Harrison, and Stu de Stael (Stuart Sutcliffe). Tommy Moore (his real name) plays the drums

Jun The Silver Beetles become The Beatles before reverting to The Silver Beetles

Jul The Silver Beetles become The Silver Beatles

12 Aug Pete Best joins The Silver Beatles as drummer

16 Aug The group finally becomes The Beatles and sets off for Hamburg

17 Aug-3 Oct The Beatles play at the Indra Club on Hamburg's Grosse Freiheit

4 Oct-30 Nov The Beatles play at the Kaiserkeller Club

15 Oct John, Paul, George, and Ringo record together for the first time, with bassist Walter Eymond of Rory Storm and the Hurricanes, at Akustic Studio, Hamburg

10 Nov John leaves Hamburg

21 Nov George is deported from West Germany for being under-age for nightclub work after midnight

29 Nov Paul and Pete are thrown into jail for apparently setting fire to their living quarters at the Bambi theater

30 Nov Paul and Pete are released from jail but deported. Stu stays in Germany with his girlfriend, Astrid Kirchherr

27 Dec The Beatles perform at the Litherland Town Hall in Liverpool, inciting the first scenes of Beatlemania

1961

9 Feb The Beatles perform for the first time at the Cavern Club, in a lunchtime session

21 Mar The Beatles perform for the first time in an evening session at the Cavern

27 Mar-2 Jul The Beatles make their second trip to Hamburg, to play at the Top Ten Club on the Reeperbahn

22-23 Jun The Beatles play in a professional recording studio for the first time, backing singer Tony Sheridan and performing a couple of numbers without him for producer Bert Kaempfert

9 Nov Brian Epstein visits the Cavern Club at lunchtime to see The Beatles performing

3 Dec The Beatles attend their first business meeting with Brian Epstein, at his record store

6 Dec Brian Epstein offers to manage the group and John accepts on their behalf

9 Dec The Beatles play their first concert down south at the Palais Ballroom, Aldershot, but it is not advertised so only 18 people turn up

13 Dec A&R man Mike Smith of Decca Records comes to see The Beatles play at the Cavern Club

1962

1 Jan The Beatles audition for Mike Smith and Dick Rowe at Decca, recording 15 songs

4 Jan The Beatles top a popularity poll in local music paper, *Mersey Beat*

24 Jan The Beatles sign a management contract with Brian Epstein, although Epstein himself does not sign

Feb Decca Records turn down The Beatles

13 Feb Brian Epstein meets George Martin, EMI Records' head of A&R, and plays him the recording of The Beatles' failed Decca audition

7 Mar The Beatles make their radio debut, recording at Manchester's Playhouse Theatre for the BBC's *Teenager's Turn (Here We Go)*, which is transmitted the following day

10 Apr Stuart Sutcliffe dies of a brain hemorrhage aged 21

13 Apr–31 May The Beatles make their third trip to Hamburg, to perform at the new Star-Club on Grosse Freiheit

9 May Brian Epstein meets George Martin again, and The Beatles are offered a recording contract, depending on an audition/recording session scheduled for Jun 6

6 Jun The Beatles perform the audition/recording session at EMI studios in Abbey Road and are formally offered a record deal

15 Aug Ringo is invited to join The Beatles and accepts

16 Aug Pete Best is sacked as The Beatles' drummer

18 Aug Ringo makes his debut as a Beatle, at Hulme Hall in Port Sunlight, Birkenhead

22 Aug The Beatles are filmed at the Cavern by Granada Television, but the footage is shelved until they become famous the following year

23 Aug John marries Cynthia Powell at Liverpool's Mount Pleasant Register Office

4 Sept The Beatles return to Abbey Road for their first formal recording session with Ringo

1 Oct Brian Epstein finally signs the management contract with The Beatles

5 Oct Their first single, "Love Me Do"/"PS I Love You," is released in the UK and reaches No. 17 in the charts

17 Oct The Beatles make their TV debut with a live appearance on Granada Television's *People And Places*, which was broadcast to the north and northwest

1-14 Nov The Beatles' fourth season in Hamburg, a two-week booking to play at the Star-Club

18-31 Dec The Beatles' fifth and final stint in Hamburg, again playing at the Star-Club

1963

2-6 Jan The Beatles travel around Scotland for their first concert tour

11 Jan Their second single, "Please Please Me"/"Ask Me Why," is released in the UK (Feb 25 in the US)

19 Jan The Beatles make their national TV debut on *Thank Your Lucky Stars*, playing "Please Please Me"

2 Feb The Beatles begin their first proper package tour of Britain, supporting Helen Shapiro

2 Feb The first London newspaper coverage of The Beatles appears in the *Evening Standard*, a general feature by Maureen Cleave

11 Feb The Beatles record ten new tracks for their first album, *Please Please Me*, in just under ten hours

19 Feb The "Please Please Me" single tops both the *New Musical Express* and *Disk* magazine charts, although it only reaches No. 2 on the BBC chart

9 Mar The Beatles embark on their second British concert tour, supporting Chris Montez and Tommy Roe

22 Mar Their first LP, *Please Please Me*, is released in the UK and tops the British charts

5 Apr The Beatles receive their first silver disk, for selling 250,000 copies of their single, "Please Please Me"

8 Apr John and Cynthia have a son, John Charles Julian

11 Apr The Beatles' third single, "From Me To You"/"Thank You Girl," is released in the UK (May 27 in the US). It is the first of eleven consecutive singles to top the British charts through to 1966

18 Apr Paul meets young actress Jane Asher after a BBC radio concert broadcast live from the Royal Albert Hall

18 May The Beatles start their third British tour

4 Jun A BBC radio series, *Pop Go The Beatles*, is launched

21 Jun "Beatle in brawl" headline appears in the *Daily Mirror*, reporting that John got drunk and beat up Cavern DJ Bob Wooler at Paul's 21st birthday party in Liverpool on Apr 18

12 Jul The EP *Twist And Shout* is released in the UK

16 Jul The Beatles record 17 songs for three separate episodes of their show, *Pop Go The Beatles* Jul 22 The LP *Introducing The Beatles* is first released in the US only. It is re-released in the US on Jan 27, 1964

1 Aug Publication of the first issue of *The Beatles Book*, a monthly magazine about the group

3 Aug The Beatles play for the last time at the Cavern Club

13 Aug The EP *Twist And Shout* sells 250,000 copies and becomes the first of its genre to qualify for silver status

23 Aug The single "She Loves You"/"I'll get You" is released in the UK (Sept 16 in the US)

3 Sept The Beatles record a further 18 songs for another three separate episodes of *Pop Go The Beatles*

6 Sept The EP *The Beatles' Hits* is released in the UK

10 Sept The Beatles receive the award for Top Vocal Group of the Year at the Variety Club Awards lunch at the Savoy hotel

15 Sept The Beatles share the bill with the Rolling Stones at the annual *Great Pop Prom* at the Royal Albert Hall

5 Oct A three-day tour of Scotland begins at the Concert Hall, Glasgow

13 Oct A live appearance by The Beatles on the network TV show, *Val Parnell's Sunday Night at the London Palladium*, causes a sensation across Britain

23 Oct The Beatles fly to Sweden for their first proper foreign concert tour

31 Oct Thousands of fans gather at London Airport to greet The Beatles on their return from Sweden

1 Nov First night of The Beatles' Autumn Tour of Britain, in Cheltenham, Gloucestershire

1 Nov The EP *The Beatles (No 1)* is released in the UK

2 Nov The *Daily Mirror* coins the term "Beatlemania," when reviewing the Cheltenham show

4 Nov The Beatles appear at the *Royal Variety Performance*, where John asks the audience to rattle their jewelry

6 Nov The footage filmed by Granada Television at the Cavern Club in 1962 is finally shown on *Scene At 6.30*

9 Nov George signs a five-year music publishing contract with Northern Songs

9 Nov After their show in East Ham, The Beatles go to a party in London given by millionaire John Bloom

16 Nov Clark's Grammar School in Guildford, Surrey becomes the first school to send boys home for sporting a Beatles haircut

22 Nov The LP *With The Beatles* is released in the UK

29 Nov The single "I Want To Hold Your Hand"/"This Boy" is released in the UK. In the US the B side is "I Saw Her Standing There" and the single is released on Dec 26

24 Dec *The Beatles' Christmas Show* begins at the Astoria Cinema, Finsbury Park, London. It runs for 16 nights

1964

3 Jan A clip of The Beatles is shown on *The Jack Paar Show* in the US

15 Jan The Beatles perform in Versailles, France, before starting a two-week season at the Olympia Theatre in Paris

20 Jan The LP *Meet The Beatles* is released in the US

25 Jan In America's *Cashbox* magazine, "I Want To Hold Your Hand" jumps 43 places to top the singles chart

30 Jan The single "Please Please Me" is re-released in the US only, with "From Me To You" as the B side

7 Feb The EP *All My Loving* is released in the UK

7 Feb The Beatles arrive at Kennedy Airport in New York

9 Feb The Beatles make a landmark television appearance on *The Ed Sullivan Show*, watched by 73 million viewers

11 Feb The Beatles' US debut concert, at the Washington Coliseum

12 Feb Two more concerts, at Carnegie Hall back in New York

12 Feb A hastily-made documentary about The Beatles' US visit is shown on UK television

13 Feb The Beatles fly from New York to Miami, to do their second *Ed Sullivan Show* and have a few days off to relax

16 Feb The second *Ed Sullivan Show* featuring The Beatles is watched by 70 million viewers

22 Feb The Beatles return to England

2 Mar A single, "Twist And Shout"/ "There's A Place," is released in the US only

2 Mar The Beatles begin shooting their first movie, *A Hard Day's Night*

10 Mar Ringo does the pub sequences for the movie in Twickenham

16 Mar The single "Can't Buy Me Love"/"You Can't Do That" is released in the US (Mar 20 in the UK)

19 Mar The Beatles collect their Variety Club of Great Britain 1963 Showbusiness Personalities of the Year award

23 Mar The Duke of Edinburgh presents The Beatles with Carl-Alan awards

23 Mar John's first book, *In His Own Write*, is published and the first print run quickly sells out

23 Mar A single, "Do You Want to Know a Secret"/"Thank You Girl," is released in the US

3 Apr The Beatles hold the top six positions in a singles chart in Sydney, Australia

4 Apr Beatles singles are also in the top five positions in America's *Billboard* chart

10 Apr An LP, *The Beatles' Second Album*, is released in the US

23 Apr John attends a Foyle's literary luncheon in his honor

27 Apr A single, "Love Me Do"/"PS I Love You," is released in the US

29 Apr The Beatles arrive in Scotland for two concerts

6 May ITV screen their own TV special, *Around The Beatles*

21 May A single, "Sie Liebt Dich"/"I'll Get You," is released in the US

May Madame Tussaud's unveil their models of The Beatles

3 Jun Ringo collapses with tonsillitis and pharyngitis just prior to The Beatles' first world tour. He is temporarily replaced by session drummer Jimmy Nicol

4 Jun The world tour begins with a concert in Copenhagen, Denmark

11 Jun The Beatles arrive in Sydney, Australia

15 Jun Ringo rejoins The Beatles in Australia and performs with them from Melbourne onwards

19 Jun The EP *Long Tall Sally* is released in the UK

26 Jun The LP *A Hard Day's Night* is released in the US (Jul 10 in the UK)

6 Jul *A Hard Day's Night* has its royal world charity première at the London Pavilion cinema

10 Jul The single, "A Hard Day's Night"/ "Things We Said Today," is released in the UK. In the US the B side is "I Should Have Known Better" and the single is released on Jul 13

12 Jul A concert at the Hippodrome, Brighton, is the first of five summer concerts at British seaside resorts

20 Jul Two singles, "I'll Cry Instead"/"I'm Happy Just to Dance With You" and "And I Love Her"/"If I Fell" are released in the US

20 Jul An LP, *Something New*, is released in the US

23 Jul The Beatles appear in a charity show, *The Night of A Hundred Stars*, at the London Palladium

18 Aug The Beatles leave London Airport for their first US concert tour

24 Aug A single, "Matchbox"/"Slow Down," is released in the US

17 Sept The Beatles are paid $150,000 to play Kansas City Municipal Stadium on their day off, earning around £1,785 per minute

9 Oct Another UK tour begins at the Gaumont Cinema, Bradford. The Beatles are joined by Motown star, Mary Wells

6 Nov The EP *Extracts From The Movie A Hard Day's Night* is released in the UK

6 Nov The EP *Extracts From The Album A Hard Day's Night* is released in the UK

8 Nov The first concert in Liverpool for nearly a year is held at the Liverpool Empire

23 Nov An LP, *The Beatles' Story*, is released in the US

23 Nov The single, "I Feel Fine"/"She's A Woman," is released in the US (Nov 27 in the UK)

1 Dec Ringo holds a Press conference about his tonsils

4 Dec The LP *Beatles For Sale* is released in the UK

15 Dec A different LP, *Beatles '65*, is released in the US

24 Dec *Another Beatles Christmas Show* begins at the Odeon, Hammersmith and runs until Jan 16, 1965

1965

11 Feb Ringo marries Mary (Maureen) Cox

12 Feb The newly-married couple hold a Press conference at the beginning of their honeymoon in Hove, East Sussex

15 Feb A single, "Eight Days a Week"/"I Don't Want to Spoil the Party," is released in the US

22 Feb The Beatles fly to the Bahamas to begin shooting their second movie, *Help!*

13 Mar After a couple of days in Britain, The Beatles fly to Austria, for more location filming

22 Mar An LP, *The Early Beatles*, is released in the US

6 Apr The EP *Beatles For Sale* is released in the UK

9 Apr The single, "Ticket To Ride"/"Yes It Is," is released in the UK (Apr 19 in the US)

14 Apr The communal house sequence for *Help!* is filmed in Ailsa Avenue, Twickenham

26 Apr Ex-Beatle Pete Best is interviewed in the *Daily Mirror*

3-5 May A sequence for *Help!* is filmed on Salisbury Plain

20 May The Beatles record their last-ever music session for BBC radio

4 Jun The EP *Beatles For Sale (No. 2)* is released in the UK

7 Jun The BBC broadcasts the last radio performance, *The Beatles (Invite You To Take A Ticket To Ride)*, which was pre-recorded on May 26

11 Jun At midnight, it is announced that The Beatles are to be awarded MBEs

14 Jun An LP, *Beatles VI*, is released in the US

20 Jun A short European concert tour of France, Italy and Spain starts with a concert in Paris

1 Jul John's second book, *A Spaniard in the Works*, is released

19 Jul The single, "Help!"/"I'm Down," is released in the US (Jul 23 in the UK)

29 Jul *Help!* has its royal world charity première at the London Pavilion

1 Aug The Beatles play live on ITV's *Blackpool Night Out*

6 Aug The LP *Help!* is released in the UK (13 Aug in the US)

15 Aug The Beatles open their second US tour with a landmark concert at New York's Shea Stadium, witnessed by a then-record audience of 55,600

27 Aug The Beatles meet Elvis Presley at his Beverly Hills home on Perugia Way

13 Sept Ringo and Maureen Starkey have a son, Zak

13 Sept A single, "Yesterday"/"Act Naturally," is released in the US

26 Oct The Beatles receive their MBEs from the Queen in the Great Throne Room at Buckingham Palace

3 Dec The Beatles start their last UK tour, playing at the Odeon Cinema, Glasgow

3 Dec The single, "We Can Work It Out"/"Day Tripper," is released in the UK (Dec 6 in the US)

3 Dec The LP *Rubber Soul* is released in the UK (Dec 6 in the US)

6 Dec The EP *The Beatles' Million Sellers* is released in the UK

17 Dec ITV broadcasts *The Music of Lennon & McCartney* around Britain, except in London where it had already been transmitted the previous evening

1966

21 Jan George marries Patricia (Pattie) Ann Boyd

8 Feb George and Pattie fly to Barbados for their honeymoon

21 Feb A single, "Nowhere Man"/"What Goes On," is released in the US

1 Mar A documentary, *The Beatles At Shea Stadium*, which was filmed in 1965 and captures Beatlemania at its peak, is shown on British television

4 Mar London's *Evening Standard* newspaper publishes an interview with John in which he states that The Beatles are "more popular than Jesus now…"

4 Mar The EP *Yesterday* is released in the UK

25 Mar The infamous "butcher" photos of The Beatles are taken by Robert Whittaker

1 May The Beatles give their last proper British concert, at Empire Pool, Wembley

21 May The Beatles are filmed in the grounds of Chiswick House in London for color promos of "Paperback Writer"/"Rain"

30 May The single, "Paperback Writer"/"Rain," is released in the US (Jun 10 in the UK)

16 Jun The Beatles' only appearance on *Top Of The Pops*, performing "Paperback Writer" and "Rain"

20 Jun An LP, *Yesterday… and Today* is released in the US, the revised version of *Yesterday And Today*, which was recalled because of complaints about the "butcher" shots on the cover

24 Jun The Beatles embark on a short tour, covering Germany, Japan and the Philippines

5 Jul The Beatles run into major problems in the Philippines after being accused of snubbing Imelda Marcos

8 Jul The EP *Nowhere Man* is released in the UK

29 Jul American teen magazine *Datebook* publishes John's *Evening Standard* interview, asserting that he said The Beatles are "greater" than Jesus.

5 Aug The single "Eleanor Rigby"/"Yellow Submarine" is released in the UK (Aug 8 in the US)

5 Aug The LP *Revolver* is released in the UK (Aug 8 in the US)

6 Aug Brian Epstein holds a Press conference in New York to explain John's "Jesus" remarks

11 Aug The Beatles fly to Chicago for their final US tour and John, supported by the others, faces the Press to explain and say he is sorry

13 Aug Radio station KLUE in Longview, Texas organizes a public "Beatles bonfire," but the next morning it is wiped off the air when a lightning bolt hits the transmission tower

29 Aug The Beatles give their very last concert at San Francisco's Candlestick Park

5 Sept John goes to Celle in West Germany to begin filming his part in *How I Won The War*

9 Nov John meets Yoko Ono for the first time when he attends a private view of her art exhibition, *Unfinished Paintings and Objects*, at London's Indica Gallery

27 Nov John movies a sequence for Peter Cook and Dudley Moore's BBC program, *Not Only...But Also*, which is shown one month later on Dec 26

9 Dec The LP *A Collection Of Beatles Oldies* is released in the UK only

1967

6 Jan The UK release of *The Family Way*, Paul's soundtrack LP of the music from the movie

27 Jan A new nine-year recording contract with EMI Records is signed by The Beatles

13 Feb The single "Strawberry Fields Forever"/"Penny Lane" is released in the US (Feb 17 in the UK)

30 Mar The famous cover photo for the *Sgt Pepper's Lonely Hearts Club Band* album is shot by Michael Cooper

19 Apr A legal business partnership, The Beatles & Co, is formed to bind the group together until 1977

20 Apr The first recording session for *Magical Mystery Tour* is held at EMI studios

15 May While attending a performance by Georgie Fame at the Bag O' Nails Club in London, Paul meets photographer Linda Eastman

19 May Brian Epstein holds a launch party for *Sgt Pepper's Lonely Hearts Club Band* at his home in London

20 May The BBC imposes a radio and TV ban on "A Day In The Life" because of the song's overt drug references

26 May The LP *Sgt Pepper's Lonely Hearts Club Band* is released in the UK before the official date of Jun 1 (Jun 2 in the US)

19 Jun Paul admits on television that he has taken LSD

24 Jun Photo-call and Press conference at Abbey Road studios for the *Our World* TV broadcast

25 Jun The Beatles perform "All You Need Is Love" on the world's first global satellite TV link-up, watched by 400,000,000. It is their last live TV performance

7 Jul The single "All You Need Is Love"/ "Baby, You're A Rich Man" is released in the UK (Jul 17 in the US)

24 Jul John, Paul, George, Ringo and Brian Epstein lend their names to a petition that is published in *The Times*, calling for the legalization of marijuana

19 Aug Ringo and Maureen have a second son, Jason

24 Aug John, George, and Paul, with wives and friends, attend a lecture by the Maharishi Mahesh Yogi at London's Hilton hotel and become interested in transcendental meditation

25 Aug The Beatles and their entourage travel to Bangor, North Wales, to attend a weekend seminar by the Maharishi

27 Aug Brian Epstein is found dead in bed at his London home

29 Aug Brian Epstein's funeral is held in Liverpool. It is a family affair and is not attended by The Beatles

1 Sept The Beatles all meet at Paul's house in St John's Wood to discuss their future

11 Sept The Beatles set off in a coach with a camera crew and 43 passengers to begin shooting on their own TV movie, *Magical Mystery Tour*

17 Oct A memorial service is held for Brian Epstein at the New London Synagogue in Abbey Road

18 Oct All The Beatles attend the première of *How I Won The War* at the London Pavilion

24 Nov The single "Hello,Goodbye"/"I Am The Walrus," is released in the UK (Nov 27 in the US)

27 Nov The LP *Magical Mystery Tour* is released in the US

3 Dec Ringo flies to Rome to begin filming his part in *Candy*

5 Dec John and George attend a party heralding the opening of The Beatles' Apple Boutique, two days later

8 Dec The EP *Magical Mystery Tour* is released in the UK

25 Dec Paul and Jane Asher announce their engagement

26 Dec BBC1 transmits the première of *Magical Mystery Tour*

27 Dec Paul appears live on *The David Frost Show* to defend *Magical Mystery Tour*

1968

25 Jan John and George attend an Ossie Clark fashion show in London, at which Pattie is one of the models

6 Feb Ringo appears live on Cilla Black's TV show, *Cilla*

15 Feb John, Cynthia, George, and Pattie fly to Rishikesh, India, to study Transcendental Meditation for three months under the Maharishi Mahesh Yogi

19 Feb Paul, Jane, Ringo, and Maureen fly out to join the others

1 Mar Ringo and Maureen have had enough and return to Britain

15 Mar The single "Lady Madonna"/"The Inner Light' is released in the UK (Mar 18 in the US)

26 Mar Paul and Jane leave for England

12 Apr John, Cynthia, George, and Pattie arrive back in London

11 May John and Paul fly to New York for five days, where they announce the setting-up of their Apple business venture

14 May John publicly denounces the Maharishi on NBC-TV's *The Tonight Show*

17 May The movie *Wonderwall*, with music by George, has its world première at the Cannes Film Festival, but it does not prove to be a box office success

22 May John and Yoko Ono appear in public together for the first time, attending a launch party and Press conference for another Apple Boutique

30 May The Black Dyke Mills Band records Paul's composition "Thingumybob" for a television series of the same name, which starts transmission on Aug 2

7 Jun Paul and Jane Asher attend Mike McCartney's wedding in North Wales

18 Jun The National Theatre's production based on John's book, *In His Own Write*, opens at the Old Vic in London

21 Jun Apple Corps buys new premises at 3 Savile Row

1 Jul John's first art exhibition, *You Are Here*, opens in London

17 Jul The Beatles' animated movie, *Yellow Submarine*, has its world première at the London Pavilion

20 Jul Jane Asher announces that her relationship with Paul is over

31 Jul The Beatles' Apple Boutique on Baker Street closes down; they also relinquish control of their second clothing store in Kings Road

22 Aug Cynthia sues John for divorce on the grounds of his adultery with Yoko Ono

23 Aug Ringo quits The Beatles during recording sessions for the *White Album*

26 Aug The single "Hey Jude"/ "Revolution" is released in the US (Aug 30 in the UK)

3 Sept Ringo rejoins The Beatles

8 Sept A pre-recorded movie clip promoting "Hey Jude" is shown on *Frost On Sunday*

30 Sept Hunter Davies' authorized biography, *The Beatles*, is first published in the UK

18 Oct John and Yoko are charged with possession of cannabis and obstructing the police

1 Nov The first solo project by a Beatle is released in the UK, *Wonderwall Music*, George's soundtrack for the movie (Dec 2 in the US)

8 Nov John and Cynthia are divorced

8 Nov George's songwriting contract with Northern Songs expires and is not renewed

11 Nov John and Yoko's album, *Unfinished Music No. 1—Two Virgins*, is released in the US (Nov 29 in the UK)

22 Nov The LP *The Beatles* (better known as the *White Album*) is released in the UK (Nov 25 in the US)

28 Nov John pleads guilty to possessing cannabis to protect Yoko

18 Dec John and Yoko appear together inside a white bag at the Royal Albert Hall

1969

2 Jan The Beatles begin filming *Get Back*, which is eventually retitled *Let It Be*

10 Jan George walks out, but is persuaded to return

13 Jan The LP *Yellow Submarine* is released in the US (Jan 17 in the UK)

30 Jan The Beatles give their last live performance on the roof of the Apple office building in central London

31 Jan For their last filmed performance, The Beatles play "The Long and Winding Road," "Let It Be" and "Two of Us"

3 Feb Allen Klein becomes The Beatles' business manager

4 Feb The New York firm of Eastman & Eastman is appointed as general counsel to Apple Corps

13 Feb Paul and Linda attend the launch of Mary Hopkin's debut album, *Postcard*

20 Feb Ringo attends the world première of *Candy* in London

1 Mar Ringo begins filming *The Magic Christian* with Peter Sellers

4 Mar Princess Margaret visits the set of *The Magic Christian* at Twickenham Studios

12 Mar Paul marries Linda Louise Eastman at Marylebone Register Office in London

12 Mar George and Pattie are busted for cannabis possession

20 Mar John marries Yoko Ono at the British Consulate in Gibraltar

25 Mar John and Yoko begin their seven-day "bed-in" for peace at the Hilton in Amsterdam, Holland

11 Apr The single "Get Back"/"Don't Let Me Down" is released in the UK (May 5 in the US)

22 Apr John formally changes his middle name to Ono during a ceremony on the roof of the Apple building

8 May Paul refuses to sign a contract appointing Allen Klein's company, ABKCO, as business manager of several of The Beatles' companies

9 May The second John and Yoko LP *Unfinished Music No 2 – Life With The Lions* is released (May 26 in the US)

9 May George releases his second solo LP *Electronic Sound* in the UK (May 26 in the US)

26 May John and Yoko begin their second "bed-in" for peace, at the Queen Elizabeth Hotel in Montreal, Canada

30 May The single "The Ballad Of John And Yoko"/"Old Brown Shoe" is released in the UK (Jun 4 in the US)

1 Jun The Plastic Ono Band, formed of John, Yoko and a selection of acquaintances, records 'Give Peace A Chance' during the "bed-in"

1 Jul Yoko and John, with her daughter Kyoko and his son Julian, are involved in a bad car crash while touring Scotland

8 Aug All four Beatles are photographed walking along the zebra crossing outside EMI studios in North London, for the cover of *Abbey Road*

20 Aug All four Beatles are together for the last time inside a recording studio, for a mix and album running order session at Abbey Road

22 Aug The Beatles are photographed together for the last time, in the grounds of John and Yoko's home, Tittenhurst Park

28 Aug A daughter, Mary, is born to Linda and Paul

28 Aug George attends a Press conference in Sydenham for the Radha Krishna Temple

1 Sept John, Yoko, George, Pattie, Ringo, and Maureen see Bob Dylan in concert at the Isle of Wight Pop Festival

13 Sept John decides to quit The Beatles, while on his way to Toronto, Canada, to perform a concert with The Plastic Ono Band

20 Sept Allen Klein negotiates an increased royalty rate for The Beatles with Capitol/EMI

26 Sept The LP *Abbey Road* is released in the UK (Oct 1 in the US)

6 Oct The Beatles single "Something"/ "Come Together" is released in the US (Oct 31 in the UK)

20 Oct The Plastic Ono Band release a single, "Cold Turkey"/"Don't Worry Kyoko (Mummy's Only Looking For Her Hand in the Snow)," in the US (Oct 24 in the UK)

20 Oct John and Yoko release *Wedding Album* in the US (Nov 7 in the UK)

25 Nov John returns his MBE to the Queen

2 Dec George joins the Delaney & Bonnie & Friends tour on stage during a concert in Bristol

10 Dec John and Yoko meet the parents of James Hanratty, as they plan to make a movie proving his innocence

11 Dec The world première of *The Magic Christian* at the Odeon, Kensington, attended by Ringo, Maureen, John, and Yoko

12 Dec Another LP, *Live Peace in Toronto*, is released by The Plastic Ono Band worldwide

14 Dec John and Yoko—or possibly two stand-ins—appear in a white bag in "A Silent Protest" about the hanging of James Hanratty

15 Dec The Plastic Ono Band, including John and George, plays a charity concert for UNICEF at the Lyceum Ballroom in London

30 Dec John is featured in a three-part ITV program, *Man of The Decade*, along with John F. Kennedy and Mao Tse Tung

1970

3-4 Jan Three Beatles, without John, participate in their last recording session during John's lifetime, performing George's song "I, Me, Mine" for the LP *Let It Be*

15 Jan *Bag One*, an exhibition of lithographs by John, opens

16 Jan John's exhibition is closed for obscenity and the police confiscate eight lithographs depicting him and Yoko

20 Jan John and Yoko have their hair cropped in Denmark

6 Feb A single, "Instant Karma"/"Who Has Seen The Wind," is released by John and Yoko in the UK (Feb 20 in the US)

26 Feb An LP, *Hey Jude*, is released in the US

6 Mar The Beatles' single "Let It Be"/ "You Know My Name (Look Up The Number)" is released in the UK (Mar 11 in the US)

12 Mar George and Pattie move into Friar Park, a mansion in Henley-on-Thames, Oxfordshire

27 Mar Ringo releases his first LP *Sentimental Journey* in the UK (Apr 24, 1970 in US)

10 Apr Newspapers around the world carry Paul's statement that The Beatles will never work together again

17 Apr Paul's first solo LP *McCartney* is released in Britain (Apr 20 in the US)

23 Apr John and Yoko go to Los Angeles to undertake a course of primal therapy with Dr. Arthur Janov

27 Apr The court declares that John's lithographs are not indecent and they are returned

8 May The Beatles LP *Let It Be* is finally released in Britain (May 18 in the US)

9 May Ringo and Maureen fly to Nice to be guests of honor at the screening of *Woodstock* at the Cannes Film Festival

11 May A Beatles single "The Long and Winding Road"/"For You Blue" is released in the US

13 May The Beatles' movie, *Let It Be*, receives its world première in New York. None of the group attends

7 Jul George's mother, Louise, dies

20 Sept George attends the opening night of "A Festival of Arts of India" at the Royal Festival Hall, London

25 Sept Ringo releases his second LP, *Beaucoups of Blues*, in the UK. (Sept 28 in the US)

15 Oct Release in the US only of Ringo's single "Beaucoups of Blues"/ "Coochy-Coochy"

11 Nov A daughter, Lee Parkin, is born to Ringo and Maureen Starkey

23 Nov George releases a single, "My Sweet Lord"/"Isn't it a Pity" in the US. (In the UK the B side is "What Is Life" and the single is released Jan 15, 1971)

27 Nov George releases his third solo LP *All Things Must Pass* in the US (Nov 30 in the UK)

8 Dec John does a major interview with *Rolling Stone*, which is published in two parts on Jan 21 and Feb 4. It is later also published as a book, *Lennon Remembers*

11 Dec John releases, *John Lennon/The Plastic Ono Band* worldwide

31 Dec Paul files a lawsuit in the London High Court to dissolve the partnership, The Beatles & Co., and appoint a receiver to handle the group's affairs

1971

19 Feb The hearing for the dissolution of The Beatles & Co. partnership commences in the London High Court

19 Feb Paul releases his first single, "Another Day"/"Oh Woman, Oh Why" in the UK (Feb 22 in the US)

23 Feb George is fined and banned from driving for a year

26 Feb Paul appears in court to give evidence in the Beatles case. The others choose not appear in person, but they do send written affidavits

12 Mar John and Yoko release a single, "Power To The People"/"Open Your Box" in the UK. In the US the B side is "Touch Me" and the single is released on Mar 22

12 Mar The High Court judge rules in favor of Paul

9 Apr Ringo's single, "It Don't Come Easy"/"Early 1970," is released in the UK (Apr 16 in the US)

15 Apr *Let it Be* wins an Oscar for Best Original Song Score

12 May Paul and his family and Ringo and Maureen go to Mick Jagger's marriage to Bianca

15 May The world première of two of John and Yoko's movies, *Apotheosis (Balloon)* and *Fly*, at the Cannes Film Festival

17 May Paul's second solo LP, *Ram*, is released in the US (May 28 in the UK)

1 Aug *A Concert For Bangladesh* is staged by George at Madison Square Garden in New York

28 Jul George releases a single, "Bangla Desh"/"Deep Blue," in the US (Jul 30 in the UK), proceeds of which go to famine relief and the homeless in Bangladesh

2 Aug Release in the US only of Paul's single, "Uncle Albert"/"Admiral Halsey b/w Too Many People"

3 Aug Paul announces the formation of his new band, Wings

13 Aug Paul's single, "Back Seat Of My Car"/"Heart Of The Country," is released in the UK only

3 Sept John and Yoko fly to New York for a short visit, which turns into a permanent stay

13 Sept A second daughter, Stella Nina, is born to Paul and Linda

8 Oct John's LP, *Imagine*, is released in the UK (Nov 9, 1971 in the US)

8 Nov Paul holds a fancy dress party at the Empire Ballroom, London, to launch Wings

10 Nov The world première of *200 Motels*, in which Ringo appears in a cameo role, is held in New York

15 Nov The world première of *Blindman*, in which Ringo appears in a cameo role, is held in Rome

23 Nov The world première of *Raga*, in which George appears in a cameo role, is held in New York

1 Dec John and Yoko release the single, "Happy Christmas (War Is Over)"/"Listen, The Snow Is Falling" in the US (Nov 24, 1972 in the UK)

4 Dec John publicly attacks Paul in the letters page of *Melody Maker*

7 Dec Paul's new band Wings release their first LP, *Wild Life* in the UK (May 22, 1980 in the US)

1972

8 Jan The triple LP of George's Bangladesh benefit concert, *The Concert For Bangla Desh*, is released in the UK (Feb 20 in the US)

9 Feb Wings start an impromptu tour of British universities by appearing unannounced at Nottingham University

25 Feb Paul releases another single, "Give Ireland Back To The Irish"/"Give Ireland Back To The Irish (version)" in the UK (Feb 28 in the US)

28 Feb George and Pattie are injured in a minor car accident in Maidenhead

17 Mar Ringo releases "Back Off Boogaloo"/"Blindman" in the UK (Mar 20 in the US)

18 Mar At the Empire Pool, Wembley, Ringo directs the filming of T. Rex in concert for the Apple movie, *Born to Boogie*

May The movie of *The Concert For Bangladesh* is shown at the Cannes Film Festival, after its world première in New York on Mar 23

12 May Wings release their first single, "Mary Had A Little Lamb"/"Little Woman Love" in the UK (May 29 in the US)

21 May BBC Radio One begins a serial, *The Beatles Story*

5 Jun George and Ravi Shankar are given an award by UNICEF in recognition of their efforts in aid of refugees in Bangladesh

12 Jun John and Yoko release their double LP, *Some Time In New York City* in the US (Sept 15 in the UK)

9 Jul Wings begin a European tour with a concert at Châteauvallon in France

10 Aug Paul and Linda are charged with possessing drugs in Sweden

30 Aug John and Yoko stage two charity concerts at Madison Square Garden in New York in aid of handicapped children

20 Sept Scottish police raid the McCartneys' farm and find cannabis plants

16 Oct Shooting of Ringo's new movie, *That'll Be the Day*, begins in the UK

1 Dec Paul releases another single, "Hi Hi Hi"/"C Moon" in the UK (Dec 4 in the US)

14 Dec Ringo attends the world première of *Born to Boogie* in London

23 Dec The world première of John and Yoko's movie, *Imagine*, on US television

1973

9 Mar Paul is fined £100 for growing five cannabis plants

18 Mar Wings play a benefit for Release at London's Hard Rock Café

23 Mar The first single from Paul and Wings, "My Love"/"The Mess" is released in the UK (Apr 9 in the US)

31 Mar Allen Klein and ABKCO reach the end of their term as business managers of Apple and other Beatles companies

2 Apr A pair of double LPs are released in the UK, *The Beatles 1962-1966* and *The Beatles 1967-1970* (Apr 19 in the US)

12 Apr The world première of *That'll Be the Day* at the ABC cinema in Shaftesbury Avenue is attended by Ringo, Maureen, Paul, and Linda

16 Apr Paul's TV movie, *James Paul McCartney*, is shown on US television (May 10 in the UK)

30 Apr Paul and Wings release an LP, *Red Rose Speedway*, in the US (May 4 in the UK)

11 May Wings begin their first proper tour of the UK with a concert in Bristol

26 May George releases a single, "Give Me Love (Give Me Peace On Earth)"/"Miss O'Dell," in the UK (May 7 in the US)

30 May George releases another LP, *Living In The Material World* in the US (Jun 22 in the UK)

1 Jun Paul releases a single of the James Bond theme that he has written, "Live And Let Die"/"I Lie Around"

4 Jul Wings start another short tour of the UK with a concert in Sheffield

5 Jul The world première of *Live and Let Die* at the Odeon, Leicester Square, attended by all of Wings

24 Sept Ringo releases his single, "Photograph"/"Down And Out" in the US (Oct 19 in the UK)

Oct John separates from Yoko and flies to Los Angeles with their secretary, May Pang

26 Oct Paul releases "Helen Wheels"/"Country Dreamer" in the UK (Nov 12 in the US)

2 Nov John, George and Ringo sue Allen Klein for misrepresentation in the High Court, and Klein counter-sues

2 Nov John releases the LP, *Mind Games* and the single, "Mind Games"/"Meat City" in the US (Nov 16, 1973 in the UK)

2 Nov Ringo releases his LP, Ringo, in the US (Nov 23 in the UK)

3 Dec Another single from Ringo, "You're Sixteen"/ "Devil Woman" is released in the US (Feb 8, 1974 in the UK)

5 Dec Paul and Wings release *Band On The Run* in the US (Dec 7 in the UK)

1974

15 Feb Release in the UK of the Paul and Wings single, "Jet"/"Let Me Roll It," from *Band On The Run* (Feb 18 in the US)

18 Feb Ringo releases his single, "Oh My My"/"Step Lightly" in the US. In the UK the B side is "No No Song" and the single is released Jan 9, 1976

8 Apr Release in the US only of the Paul and Wings single "Band on the Run"/ "Nineteen Hundred and Eighty Five"

28 Jun Release in the UK only of the Paul and Wings single, "Band On The Run"/"Zoo Gang," from *Band On The Run*

23 Sept John releases his single, "Whatever Gets You Through The Night"/"Beef Jerky," in the US (Oct 4 in the UK)

26 Sept John releases his LP, *Walls And Bridges* in the US (Oct 4 in the UK)

18 Oct UK release of "Walking in the Park with Eloise"/ "Bridge Over the River Suite," by the Country Hams, a pseudonym for Paul and Wings with Floyd Cramer and Chet Atkins (Dec 2 in the US)

25 Oct Paul releases his single, "Junior's Farm"/"Sally G" in the UK (Nov 4 in the US)

28 Oct Allen Klein loses his court case against John, George, and Ringo

2 Nov George begins his solo tour of the US with a concert at the Pacific Coliseum, Vancouver

11 Nov Ringo releases his single, "Only You"/"Call Me" in the US (Nov 15 in the UK)

15 Nov Ringo releases his LP, *Goodnight Vienna* in the UK (Nov 18 in the US)

16 Nov John has his first solo No. 1 in the US, when "Whatever Gets You Through The Night" reaches the top of the *Billboard* chart

18 Nov George releases his single, "Dark Horse"/"I Don't Care Anymore" in the US only. In the UK the B side is "Hari's on Tour (Express)" and the single is released on Feb 28, 1975

6 Dec George releases his single, "Ding Dong"/"I Don't Care Anymore" in the UK only

9 Dec George releases his LP, *Dark Horse* in the US (Dec 20 in the UK)

16 Dec First US release of John's single, "#9 Dream"/"What You Got" (Jan 31, 1975 in the UK)

1975

Jan John returns to Yoko in New York

9 Jan The Beatles & Co. partnership is formally dissolved in the London High Court

16 Jan Wings begin to record for their next album, *Venus and Mars*

27 Jan Release in the US only of Ringo's single "No No Song"/"Snookeroo"

7 Feb Paul and Wings' single, "Junior's Farm"/"Sally G" is re-issued in the UK only, with the A and B sides swopped round

17 Feb John releases his LP, *Rock 'n' Roll* in the US (Feb 21 in the UK)

21 Feb Release in the UK only of Ringo's single "Snookeroo"/"Oo Wee"

1 Mar John and Yoko appear together again in public, at the Grammy Awards in the US, where John is a guest presenter

3 Mar Linda is arrested and charged in the US with possession of cannabis

6 Mar John issues a statement that his separation from Yoko is over

10 Mar John releases a single, "Stand By Me"/ "Move Over Ms L' in the US (Apr 18 in the UK)

24 Mar Capitol Records in the US holds a party for Wings on the liner *Queen Mary*, which is docked at Long Beach

26 Mar Ringo attends the London première of the movie *Tommy* with his new girlfriend, Nancy Andrews

16 May UK release of Paul and Wings' single, "Listen to What the Man Said"/"Love in Song" (May 23 in the US)

30 May UK release of the Paul and Wings album, *Venus and Mars*

17 Jul Ringo and Maureen Starkey are divorced

5 Sept Release in the UK of Wings' single, "Letting Go"/"You Gave Me the Answer" (Sept 29 in the US)

9 Sept Wings begin a world tour with a concert at the Gaumont Cinema in Southampton

3 Oct George releases his LP, *Extra Texture (Read All About it)* in the UK (Dec 22 in the US)

7 Oct The New York State Senate votes to reverse the deportation order against John, which he has been fighting for some years

9 Oct A son, Sean Taro Ono, is born to John and Yoko

10 Oct The world première in New York of *Lisztomania*, which includes a cameo appearance by Ringo

24 Oct First release in the UK only of John's single, "Imagine"/"Working Class Hero"

1 Nov Wings continue their world tour, with a concert in Perth

21 Nov Linda's US drug charge is dismissed

25 Nov Ringo releases his LP *Blast From Your Past* in the US (Dec 12 in the UK)

28 Nov First UK release of the Paul and Wings single "Venus and Mars"/"Rock Show"

8 Dec George releases his single, "This Guitar (Can't keep from Crying)"/"Maya Love" in the US (Feb 6, 1976 in the UK)

1976

25 Jan Ringo appears with Bob Dylan in a benefit concert for Rubin "Hurricane" Carter in Houston

26 Jan The Beatles' recording contract with EMI expires. Paul stays with EMI, but George and Ringo move to other labels. John does not sign with anyone

5 Mar EMI releases a boxed set of all the original UK Beatles singles, as well as re-releasing them all individually, with one new issue, "Yesterday"

20 Mar Paul and Wings continue their world tour with several concerts in Europe, starting in Copenhagen, Denmark

26 Mar Paul and Wings release their LP, *Wings at the Speed of Sound* in the UK only

1 Apr Paul and Wings release their single, "Silly Love Songs"/ "Cook of the House" in the US (Apr 30 in the UK)

3 May Paul and Wings begin touring the US and Canada, with a concert at Fort Worth

23 Jun Paul and Wings complete their world tour with three nights at the Forum, Los Angeles. Ringo joins them on stage during the final song of their encore and gives Paul a bunch of flowers

28 Jun Paul and Wings release their single, "Let 'em In"/ "Beware My Love" in the US (Jul 23 in the UK)

27 Jul John finally gets his Green Card

7 Sept George is found guilty of plagiarizing "He's So Fine" for his hit song, "My Sweet Lord"

7 Sept After buying the rights to Buddy Holly's songs, Paul stages the first Buddy Holly Week in London, which becomes an annual event

17 Sept Ringo releases his LP, *Ringo's Rotogravure* (Sept 27 in the US)

19 Sept Paul and Wings begin a short tour of Europe with a concert in Vienna

20 Sept Ringo releases his single, "A Dose of Rock and Roll"/"Cryin' in the US (Oct 15 in the UK)

15 Nov George releases his single, "This Song"/"Learning How to Love You" in the US (Nov 19 in the UK)

19 Nov George releases his LP, *33 1/3* worldwide

22 Nov Ringo releases his single "Hey Baby"/"Lady Gaye" in the US (Nov 29 in the UK)

10 Dec Paul and Wings release their triple LP, *Wings Over America* in the UK

1977

10 Jan All outstanding litigation between Allen Klein and The Beatles is settled

4 Feb Wings release their single "Maybe I'm Amazed" in the UK, a live version of Paul's original solo version

11 Feb George releases his single, "True Love"/"Pure Smokey" in the UK

4 Apr The Beatles go to the High Court to stop the release of an LP recorded live in Hamburg in 1962; the judge decrees it can be released

29 Apr First release in the UK of the LP *Thrillington*, by Percy "Thrills" Thrillington, pseudonym of Paul McCartney (May 17 in the US)

4 May The live LP, *The Beatles at the Hollywood Bowl*, is released in the US (May 6 in the UK)

25 May *The Beatles Live! At the Star-Club in Hamburg, Germany, 1962* is released in the UK (Jun 13 in the US)

31 May Linda and Wings release a single, "Seaside Woman," in the US under the pseudonym Suzy and the Red Stripes. It is released in the UK on Aug 10, 1979

9 Jun George and Pattie are divorced

12 Sept A son, James Louis, is born to Paul and Linda

16 Sept Ringo releases his single, "Drowning in a Sea of Love"/"Just a Dream" in the UK (Oct 18 in the US)

26 Sept US release of Ringo's LP, *Ringo the 4th* (Sept 30 in UK)

11 Nov Paul and Wings release their single, "Mull of Kintyre"/"Girl's School" in the UK

1978

14 Jan The first of LWT's *The South Bank Show* features Paul, with an interview and exclusive footage

22 Mar Paul and Wings hold a Press conference during a Thames boat trip to promote their new LP, *London Town*

20 Mar Paul and Wings release their single, "With a Little Luck"/"Backwards Traveller – Cuff Link" in the US (Mar 24 in the UK)

31 Mar Official UK release of the Paul and Wings" LP, *London Town*

21 Apr Ringo releases his LP, *Bad Boy* in the US (Jun 16 in the UK)

26 Apr Ringo appears in his own TV special, *Ringo*, on US television, with George making a cameo appearance. It is not shown in the UK until Jan 2, 1983

12 Jun Paul and Wings release their single, "I've Had Enough"/"Deliver Your Children" in the US (Jun 16 in the UK)

21 Jul Ringo releases his single, "Tonight"/"Old Time Relovin" in the UK

1 Aug A son, Dhani, is born to George and his girlfriend, Olivia Arias

11 Aug First UK release of Wings' single "London Town"/"I'm Carrying" (Aug 21 in the US)

2 Sept George & Olivia marry

1979

14 Feb George releases his single, "Blow Away"/"Soft Hearted Hana' in the US. In the UK the B side is "Soft Touch" and the single is released two days later on Feb 16

14 Feb US release of George's LP, *George Harrison* (Feb 16 in the UK)

16 Feb George releases his single, "Blow Away"/"Soft Touch" in the UK. In the US the A side is "Love Comes To Everyone" and the single is released on May 11

15 Mar Wings release their single, "Goodnight Tonight"/"Daytime Night-time Suffering" in the US (Mar 23 in the UK)

Apr Ringo nearly dies from severe intestinal problems but has an operation in Monte Carlo

27 Apr Allen Klein is found guilty of tax evasion in New York and is sent to prison

19 May Paul, George and Ringo reunite for a jam session at a garden party celebrating the marriage of Eric Clapton to the former Pattie Harrison

8 Jun UK release of Paul and Wings' LP, *Back to the Egg*, which is followed by a big party on the Jun 11 at EMI's Abbey Road studios

13 Jul George releases his single "Faster"/"Your Love Is Forever" in the UK

10 Aug Paul and Wings release their single, "Getting Closer"/"Baby's Request" in the UK

22 Aug George publishes an autographed, limited edition book, *I Me Mine*. All 2,000 copies sell out quickly, despite the price of £148

24 Oct The Guinness Book of Records presents Paul with a rhodium disk

16 Nov Paul releases a single, "Wonderful Christmastime"/ "Rudolf the Red-Nosed Reggae" in the UK (Nov 20 in the US)

24 Nov Wings begin a UK tour with the first of three concerts in Liverpool

28 Nov All Ringo's Beatles mementoes are destroyed when his house in the Hollywood Hills is burnt down

7&10 Dec Wings play two nights at the Empire Pool, Wembley as part of their UK tour

29 Dec Wings play in a concert for Kampuchean refugees and UNICEF at the Odeon, Hammersmith. Paul also gathers together a massive collection of musicians to form his "Rockestra" to play three numbers

1980

16 Jan Arriving in Japan to begin a tour, Paul is arrested for carrying cannabis

18 Feb Ringo begins shooting *Caveman* in Mexico

26 Feb Paul receives the Outstanding Music Personality award at the British Rock and Pop Music Awards at the Café Royal

27 Feb Paul's "Rockestra Theme" wins a Grammy award

11 Apr Paul releases his single, "Coming Up"/"Coming Up (live)—Lunch Box-Odd Sox" in the UK (Apr 15 in the US)

9 May Yul Brynner presents Paul with a Special Ivor Novello Award for his services to British music

16 May UK release of Paul's LP, *McCartney II* (May 21 in the US)

19 May Ringo and his new girlfriend Barbara Bach are involved in a serious car crash in London, but escape without injury

13 Jun Paul releases his single, "Waterfalls"/ "Check My Machine" in the UK (Jul 22 in the US)

1 Aug George forms his own movie company, HandMade Films (Productions) Ltd

9 Sept John and Yoko start an interview session for *Playboy* magazine, which lasts nearly 19 days

15 Sept UK release of Paul's single, "Temporary Secretary"/"Secret Friend"

22 Sept Yoko signs a record deal for herself and John with Geffen Records

29 Sept The first interview with John and Yoko for several years is published in *Newsweek*

24 Oct First UK release of John's single, "(Just Like) Starting Over"/"Kiss Kiss Kiss" (Oct 27 in the US)

17 Nov John and Yoko release their new LP, *Double Fantasy* in the US and UK

26 Nov The world première of *Rockshow*, a movie of Wings' 1976 tour of the US, is held in New York

5 Dec John tapes an interview for the magazine *Rolling Stone*

6 Dec John and Yoko together record an interview for BBC Radio One

8 Dec John and Yoko together record an interview for RKO Radio

8 Dec John is shot dead at the age of 40 by a deranged fan outside his apartment in New York

14 Dec Ten minutes of silence is observed at 7.00 pm GMT around the world in memory of John

1981

12 Jan US release of John's single, "Woman"/"Beautiful Boys" (Jan 16 in the UK)

23 Feb The LP *The McCartney Interview* is released as a limited edition in the UK and deleted the same day

26 Feb George is ordered to pay $587,000 in damages for his unconscious plagiarizing of "He's So Fine." The money goes to Bright Tunes, owned by Allen Klein

13 Mar US release of John's single, "Watching the Wheels"/"Yes, I'm Your Angel" (Mar 27 in the UK)

8 Apr Paul and Linda attend the UK charity première of *Rockshow* in London

10 Apr The world première of *Caveman* is held in New York; the movie is not a success

27 Apr Ringo marries Barbara Bach in London

27 Apr Wings officially split

11 May George's tribute to John, "All Those Years Ago," featuring backing by Paul and Ringo, is released as a single in the US. The B side is "Writing's on the Wall" (May 15 in the UK)

27 May George releases his LP *Somewhere in England* in the US (Jun 5 in the UK)

31 Jul UK release of George's single "Teardrops"/"Save the World." In the US "All Those Years Ago" is re-issued, with "Teardrops" now on the B side (Nov 4)

28 Sept A book that includes Paul's music, lyrics and drawings, *Paul McCartney: Composer/Artist* is published in the UK

27 Oct Ringo releases his single, "Wrack My Brain"/"Drumming is my Madness" in the US (Nov 13 in the UK)

27 Oct US release of Ringo's LP *Stop and Smell the Roses* (Nov 20 in the UK)

1982

11 Jan Paul's MPL Company starts shooting *The Cooler*, to promote three tracks from Ringo's LP *Stop and Smell the Roses*. Paul, Linda, Ringo and Barbara all appear

30 Jan Paul appears on *Desert Island Disks*, for BBC Radio Four

24 Feb Yoko and Sean attend the Grammy presentations in the US to collect the Best Album award for *Double Fantasy*

7 Mar The BBC's Radio One network celebrates the 20th anniversary of The Beatles' first broadcast with a two-hour show called Beatles at the Beeb. It is broadcast in the US on May 31, 1982

22 Mar A single, "The Beatles Movie Medley"/"I'm Happy Just to Dance With You" is released in the US (May 24 in the UK)

26 Mar UK release of the single "Ebony and Ivory" by Paul with Stevie Wonder, with "Rainclouds" by Paul only on the B side (Apr 2 in the US)

26 Apr Paul releases his LP Tug of War in the US and UK

21 Jun Paul releases his single "Take It Away"/"I'll Give You a Ring" in the UK (Jul 3 in the US)

20 Sept The UK release of Paul's single "Tug of War"/"Get It" (Sept 26 in the US)

18 Oct UK release of a compilation album, *The Beatles: 20 Greatest Hits*

25 Oct US and UK release of "The Girl is Mine," with Paul and Michael Jackson and "Can't Get Outta the Rain" by Michael only on the B side

29 Oct George releases his single "Wake Up My Love"/"Greece" in the UK

1 Nov UK release of *The John Lennon Collection*, a compilation LP (Nov 8 in the US)

15 Nov In the UK, EMI issue John's "Love" as a single for the first time, with "Give Me Some Truth" on the B side

27 Oct US release of George's LP *Gone Troppo* (Nov 8 in the UK)

8 Nov Paul's movie, *Give My Regards to Broad Street*, starts filming at Elstree with Paul, Linda, and Ringo starring

1983

4 Jun A 26-part series, Ringo's *Yellow Submarine: A Voyage Through Beatles Magic*, begins on US radio, with Ringo telling the story of the group

16 Jun Ringo's LP *Old Wave* is released in West Germany. It is also issued in Canada and Brazil but no US or UK record company will take it

18 Jul In Studio Two at Abbey Road, EMI shows *The Beatles at Abbey Road*, with rare video footage and recording session tapes. It runs for nearly two months and fans travel from all over the world

3 Oct UK release of "Say Say Say" by Paul with Michael Jackson

17 Oct Paul releases his LP *Pipes of Peace* in the UK (Oct 26 in the US)

6-7 Oct Ringo and Barbara appear in *Princess Daisy* on US television

5 Dec Paul releases his single "Pipes of Peace" in the UK

5 Dec US release of *Heart Play—Unfinished Dialogue*, an LP with bits of John and Yoko's 1980 interview for *Playboy* magazine (Dec 16 in the UK)

1984

5 Jan US release of John's single "Nobody Told Me"/"O'Sanity" (Jan 9 in the UK)

16 Jan John and Linda are arrested in Barbados for possession of cannabis

17 Jan Linda is arrested again at Heathrow when small amount of cannabis is found in her luggage when she and Paul return to London

19 Jan US release of John and Yoko's LP *Milk and Honey* (Jan 23 in the UK)

9 Mar UK release of John's single "Borrowed Time"/"Your Hands" (May 11 in the US)

15 Mar US release of John's single "I'm Stepping Out"/"Sleepless Night" (Jul 15 in the UK)

21 Mar A plot of land in Central Park bought by Yoko is dedicated to John and named Strawberry Fields

Apr An unauthorized double LP, *Reflections and Poetry*, containing part of the interview John gave to RKO Radio before he died, is released in the UK, but is withdrawn after Yoko takes legal action. The full interview is released as *The Last Word* in the UK in Jul 1988

7 Sept As part of the eighth Buddy Holly Week, Paul presents the prizes at a Holly drawing competition in London

24 Sept Paul releases his single "No More Lonely Nights" in the UK

5 Oct US release of John's single "Every Man Has a Woman Who Loves Him" with "It's Alright" sung by Sean Lennon on the B side (Nov 16 in the UK)

9 Oct A series of *Thomas the Tank Engine and Friends*, read by Ringo, is first transmitted on ITV

14 Oct LWT's *The South Bank Show* is dedicated to *Give My Regards to Broad Street*

22 Oct UK and US release of the soundtrack LP *Give My Regards to Broad Street*

25 Oct The world première of *Give My Regards to Broad Street* is held in New York and Paul and Linda attend

12 Nov Paul releases his single "We All Stand Together"/ "We All Stand Together (humming version)" in the UK only

28 Nov In the afternoon, Paul attends a ceremony to receive the Freedom of the City of Liverpool. In the evening, the UK première of *Give My Regards to Broad Street* is held in Liverpool with *Rupert and the Frog Song* as supporting picture

29 Nov The London première of *Give My Regards to Broad Street* is held at the Odeon, Leicester Square, attended by Paul, Linda, Ringo, Barbara and Olivia Harrison.

14 Dec George makes an unannounced appearance with Deep Purple at their concert in Sydney

1985

18 Jan The world première of *Water*, made by HandMade Films, is held in London. George and Ringo both have cameo roles

26 Jan George plays guitar for a musical version of *The Hunting of the Snark*, by Lewis Carroll

11 Mar Ringo appears in *Willie and the Poor Boys* in a cameo role

13 Jul Paul appears in the Live Aid concert for famine relief in Ethiopia

10 Aug Michael Jackson acquires the rights to all the Lennon-McCartney songs when he buys Northern Songs for $47.5 million

7 Sept Ringo becomes the first Beatle grandfather, when his eldest son Zak and wife Sarah have their first child, a girl named Tatia Jane.

12 Oct Ringo and Barbara attend the Chelsea Arts Club Ball in London

18 Nov Paul releases his single "Spies Like Us" in the UK

18 Nov First UK release of John's 1971 song "Jealous Guy"/"Going Down On Love" as a single. It is released in the US with "Give Peace a Chance" as the B side on Sept 19, 1988

9 Dec Ringo appears as the Mock Turtle in *Alice in Wonderland* on US television

1986

1 Jan A TV special, *Blue Suede Shoes: Carl Perkins and Friends*, is shown on UK's Channel 4 for the first time. Both George and Ringo perform in tribute

24 Jan US release of the LP *John Lennon: Live in New York City* (Feb 24 in the UK)

26 Jan George attends the London *Standard* Film Awards at the Savoy hotel in London, where HandMade Films picks up several awards Jan27 Paul receives an Award of Merit in the American Music Awards

6 Mar George holds a Press conference at the close of shooting of *Shanghai Surprise*, along with the movie's star, Madonna

15 Mar George appears at a benefit concert for a local children's hospital at the National Exhibition Centre in Birmingham, England

21 Mar Yoko appears at Wembley Conference Centre as part of her Star Peace world tour, which covered 33 cities in seven weeks

14 Jul Paul releases his single "Press" in the UK

22 Aug US release of Paul's LP *Press to Play* (Sept 1 in the UK)

29 Aug A BBC TV special, *McCartney*, features extensive new interviews with Paul

29 Aug World première in the US of *Shanghai Surprise* by HandMade Films, for which George has done the soundtrack and appeared in a cameo role

3 Sept Paul and Linda attend the opening of a photographic exhibition on the British countryside at London's Royal Festival Hall

16 Oct The video of *Rupert and the Frog Song* picks up the 1985 Best Selling Video award at the British Video Awards held at the Grosvenor House hotel in London.

27 Oct Paul releases his single "Pretty Little Head" in the UK

27 Oct US release of the LP *Menlove Avenue*, which contains previously unreleased recordings by John (Nov 3 in the UK)

24 Nov Paul makes a surprise appearance at the Royal Variety Performance, which is televised on BBC 1 on Nov 29

1 Dec Paul releases his single "Only Love Remains" in the UK

1987

26 Feb The first four official Beatles compact disks, Please Please Me, With The Beatles, A Hard Day's Night and Beatles For Sale, are released by EMI in the UK

1 Jun On the 20th anniversary of the official release date of *Sgt Pepper's Lonely Hearts Club Band*, Granada Television screens a two-hour documentary called *It Was Twenty Years Ago Today*, featuring interviews with Paul and George. Paul and Linda attend a party to celebrate the event

5-6 Jun George plays two concerts for the Prince's Trust at Wembley, with guests including Eric Clapton, Ringo and Phil Collins

12 Oct UK release of George's single, "Got My Mind Set on You"/"Lay His Head" (Oct 16 in the US)

17 Oct George joins Bob Dylan for two songs of the encore during his concert at Wembley

2 Nov After a five-year break from recording, George releases his LP/CD *Cloud Nine* in the US and UK

2 Nov Release of Paul's CD *All The Best*, with a selection of his finest post-Beatles hits (Dec 5, 1987 in the US)

16 Nov Release in the UK of Paul's single "Once Upon a Long Ago"/"Back on My Feet"

16 Nov A series of cassettes of *Thomas the Tank Engine* stories, with narration by Ringo, are released in the UK

1988

20 Jan George, Ringo, Yoko and Julian and Sean Lennon attend the awards ceremony at the Waldorf Astoria in New York, when The Beatles are added to the Rock and Roll Hall of Fame

25 Jan US and UK release of George's single, "When We Was Fab"/"Zig Zag"

2 May US release of George's single, "This is Love"/ "Breath Away From Heaven"

11 Jul Release of the CD *The Last Word* in the UK only, consisting of part of the interview with John at RKO radio made hours before his death

Sept Release of "T-shirt," a new single by Buddy Holly's old supporting group, The Crickets, which Paul has produced

30 Sept UK release of Paul's CD *Choba B CCCP* (Back in The USSR) a collection of Rock and Roll classics originally intended only for the Russian market (Oct 29 in the US)

4 Oct US release of the CD/LP *Imagine: John Lennon* (Oct 10 in the UK)

17 Oct US release of the Traveling Wilburys' single, "Handle With Care"/ "Margarita"

18 Oct First release in the US of the Traveling Wilburys' CD/LP *The Traveling Wilburys Volume One* (Oct 24 in the UK)

1989

21 Mar US release of a boxed Gift Set of Paul's earlier LPs, *McCartney*, *Ram*, *Red Rose Speedway* and *McCartney II* (May 2 in the UK)

5 Jun Paul releases a new LP/CD, *Flowers in the Dirt* in the UK (Jun 6 in the US)

23 Jul Ringo and his All-Starr Band play a concert in Dallas to begin their 1989 world tour

26 Jul Paul introduces his new backing band at the first of two concerts at the London Playhouse Theatre

24 Aug US release of George's single "Cheer Down"/"That's What It Takes"

23-29 Nov While appearing in Los Angeles during his world tour, Paul meets up again with Michael Jackson backstage after the show

19 Dec Paul receives an award for his contribution to pop music from the Performing Right Society

1990

2-26 Jan As part of his continuing world tour, Paul plays six nights at the International Arena in Birmingham, UK and eleven nights at Wembley Arena

1 Feb Release of Paul's *World Tour Special Edition* CD

21 Feb Paul receives a Lifetime Achievement Grammy Award

1 May George appears in Los Angeles with Eric Clapton during the Journeyman tour

28 Jun Paul and his band give a concert for charity in Liverpool as part of their world tour

5 Oct George joins the Gary Moore concert on stage to play guitar

8 Oct Ringo releases a CD *Ringo Starr and His All-Starr Band* in the UK (Oct 12 in the US)

5 Nov US and UK release of Paul's double-CD/triple-LP *Tripping the Live Fantastic*, featuring music from the 1989/90 tour

19 Nov UK and US release of Paul's CD *Tripping the Live Fantastic—Highlights*, a condensed version of the 1989/90 tour

1991

20 May Release in the UK of Paul's CD *Unplugged: The Official Bootleg*, a performance taped during a show in 1991 and released in a limited edition of 250,000 copies (Jun 4 in the US)

28 Jun The world première of Paul's *Liverpool Oratorio*, by Paul and Carl Davis, is held at the Anglican cathedral in Liverpool

22 Oct US release of the album of *Paul McCartney's Liverpool Oratorio*

11 Nov Both UK and US release of Paul's single "Save The Child"

1992

3 Apr Ringo is a guest presenter at the Grammy Awards in the US

6 Apr George plays a benefit concert for The Natural Law Party at the Royal Albert Hall in London, with Ringo making a special guest appearance

22 May Ringo releases his CD *Time Takes Time* in the US (Jun 29 in the UK)

2 Jun Ringo and his All-Starr Band do a concert in Fort Lauderdale, Florida to kick off their world tour

13 Jul UK release of George's CD *Live in Japan*, recorded during the tour of 1991 (Jul 14 in the US)

1993

18 Jan Both UK and US release of Paul's EP, *Hope of Deliverance*

5 Feb Paul begins another world tour with a concert in Docklands, London

2 Feb Release of Paul's LP/CD *Off the Ground* in the UK (Feb 9 in the US)

14 Sept Ringo releases his CD *Ringo Starr and His All-Starr Band: Live at Montreux* recorded live at the Jazz Festival in Jul 1992

16 Nov US and UK release of Paul's CD *Paul is Live*, with 24 live tracks including two previously unreleased new songs. It is also issued as an LP in the UK only

1994

19 Jan John is installed as a solo artiste in the Rock and Roll Hall of Fame in Cleveland, Ohio

30 Nov The two-CD set, *The Beatles—Live At The BBC*, is released in the UK (Dec 6 in the US)

1995

14 Jun Ringo and his All-Starr Band play a concert in Morioka, Japan, to begin their 1995 world tour

19 Nov The three-part, six-hour documentary, *The Beatles Anthology*, begins on ABC-TV in the US. It is shown in six parts in the UK in Dec

21 Nov The double LP, *The Beatles Anthology 1*, is released worldwide

4 Dec The Beatles single "Free As A Bird" is released in the UK (Dec 12 in the US)

1996

4 Mar The second new Beatles single, "Real Love," is released in the UK (Mar 12 in the US)

18 Mar The double LP, *The Beatles Anthology 2*, is released in the UK (Mar 19 in the US)

28 Oct The double LP, *The Beatles Anthology 3*, is released in the UK (Oct 29 in the US)

1997

26 Feb The Beatles receive a total of three Grammy Awards, two for "Free As A Bird" and one for *The Beatles Anthology*

11 Mar Paul receives his knighthood from the Queen

6 May Release of Paul's single "The World Tonight"/ "Looking For You" in the US

27 May US release of Paul's LP/CD *Flaming Pie*

12 Aug US release of *Ringo Starr and His Third All-Starr Band* recorded live in 1995 in Tokyo

23 Sept US release of Paul's classical music album, *Standing Stone*

1998

17 Apr Linda dies of breast cancer

20 Oct Ringo releases a CD *VH1 Storytellers* in the US, on which he tells the story behind each song before it is performed

2 Nov Release in the UK of the 4-CD *The John Lennon Anthology*, containing more than 100 previously unreleased tracks (Nov 3 in the US)

2 Nov UK release of the CD *Wonsaponatime*, containing selected tracks from *The John Lennon Anthology* (Nov 3 in the US)

1999

15 Mar Paul is included in the Rock and Roll Hall of Fame as a solo artiste

1 Aug The Aug issue of the UK magazine *Q* publishes a readers' poll of the 100 Greatest Stars of the 20th Century, in which John comes first, with Paul second

14 Sept Release in the UK and US of a compilation album, *Yellow Submarine Songtrack*, of all the Beatles songs featured in the film. It is released in conjunction with a restored version of the film itself

4 Oct Release of Paul's LP/CD *Run Devil Run* in the UK, with Paul covering rock 'n' roll classics along with a couple of new songs (Oct 5 in the US)

16 Oct World première of Paul's *Working Classical* in Liverpool, which is performed by the London Symphony Orchestra

30 Dec George is stabbed, and his wife, Olivia, injured, in the early hours of the morning by an intruder in his home at Henley-on-Thames

2000

13 Nov Official launch of TheBeatles.com, a web site featuring all the No. 1 hits

2001

Apr A cancer-like sore is removed from George's lungs at the Mayo Clinic in Rochester, Minn.

May Paul releases *Wingspan: Hits & History*, a compilation album of Wings' greatest hits

24 Jul UK release of Ringo's *The Anthology…So Far*, a 3-CD set of live material

26 Jul Ringo's All-Starr Band begins a tour of North America

20 Oct Paul joins David Bowie, Mick Jagger and other major rock stars in Concert for New York, a benefit after the Sep 11 terrorist attack on the city

Nov At Staten Island University Hospital in New York, George has experimental radiosurgery for a brain tumor

13 Nov Paul releases his album, *Driving Rain*

19 Nov Release of Jools Holland's album, *Small World, Big Friends*, featuring "A Horse to Water" recorded by George with his son Dhani

29 Nov George dies of cancer at the home of a friend in Los Angeles

2002

11 Jun Paul marries Heather Mills at Castle Leslie in Ireland

6 Aug Ringo releases his live album, *King Biscuit Flower Presents Ringo & His New All-Starr Band*

18 Nov George's album *Brainwashed* released. Incomplete at the time he died, the album was finished by his son Dhani and Jeff Lynne.

29 Nov Paul and Ringo perform at the Concert for George held at the Royal Albert Hall in London with Eric Clapton and Billy Preston

2003

17 Mar Paul releases his album *Back in the World Live*

17 Nov *Let It Be…Naked* is released

2004

15 Mar George is inducted into the Rock and Roll Hall of Fame

2 Jul Paul performs at the Live 8 charity concert in Hyde Park

2005

4 Oct Paul's single "Jenny Wren" is released and later nominated in 2007 Grammy Awards for Best Male Pop Vocal Performance

21 Nov *Working Class Hero: the Definitive Lennon* album is released

2006

17 May Paul and Heather announce their separation

20 Nov The Beatles Love album released in UK and USA—comprising remixes by George Martin and son Giles of 26 Beatles classics, providing music for Cirque du Soleil's Las Vegas show.

2007

5 Feb Apple Inc. and Apple Corps announce a settlement of their trademark dispute

21 Mar Leaving EMI, Paul is the first artist to sign to Starbucks' new record label, Hear Music.

Nov Paul begins dating Nancy Shevell

2008

10 Feb The *Love* album wins two Grammy Awards—Best Compilation Soundtrack Album and Best Surround Sound Album

24 Mar Neil Aspinall dies of lung cancer; Jeff Jones takes over as head of Apple Corps after leaving Sony BMG

10 Jul Beatles Day is inaugurated in Liverpool, marking their triumphal return to the city that day in 1964

2009

15 Jul Over 45 years after The Beatles first appeared on American television on *The Ed Sullivan Show*, McCartney returns to the Ed Sullivan Theater, performing live to a street audience, watched over by David Letterman.

9 Sept *The Beatles Rock Band* interactive computer game is released; On the same day, remastered versions of the band's twelve original studio albums plus *Magical Mystery Tour* and the compilation, *Past Masters*, are issued as *The Beatles Stereo Box Set*; remastered mono recordings are simultaneously released as *The Beatles in Mono*.

2010

8 Feb Ringo is honored with the 2,401st star on the Hollywood Walk of Fame

Bibliography

The Beatles – Hunter Davies (London, Arrow Books, 1992)

The Beatles: 25 Years in the Life, A Chronology 1962-1987 – Mark Lewisohn (London, Sidgwick & Jackson, 1987)

The Beatles Files – Andy Davis (UK, Color Library Direct, 1998)

The Complete Beatles Chronicle – Mark Lewisohn (London, Hamlyn, 1992)

The Complete Idiot's Guide to The Beatles – Richard Buskin (New York, Alpha Books, 1998)

The Love You Make – Peter Brown & Steven Gaines (London, Macmillan, 1983)

Acknowledgements

The Photographs from this book were taken by
Associated Newspapers' photographers and are from the archives of the Daily Mail.

Many of these fabulous photographs, taken by some of the world's leading professionals, are from negatives never previously printed. The photographers' work has been carefully archived by the very dedicated staff in the Picture Library resulting in one of the last great remaining photographic treasures chronicling The Beatles. The pleasure this book will give to the fans of the greatest rock band of the twentieth century is a tribute to the continued diligence and hard work of the team. Many thanks to Alan Pinnock, David Sheppard and the present staff and all those who have held this important responsibility before them.

Thanks also to Christine Hoy, John Dunne, Cliff Salter Paul Rossiter, Richard Betts, Keith Lock, Ian Withers, Alan Hatherly and Alison Gauntlett.

Particular thanks to Steve Torrington without whom this book would not have been possible.

Finally, thanks to the late Sir David English
who was so inspirational and who would have enjoyed seeing the finished book.